you can't ruin my day

52 Wake-Up Calls to
Turn Any Situation Around

Allen Klein

Foreword by Kristine Carlson

VIVA
EDITIONS

Published in the United States by Viva Editions, an imprint of Start Midnight, LLC, 375 Hudson Street, Twelfth Floor, New York, New York 10014.

Printed in the United States.
Cover design: Scott Idleman/Blink
Text design: Frank Wiedemann
First Edition.
10 9 8 7 6 5 4 3 2 1

Trade paper ISBN: 978-1-63228-022-0
E-book ISBN: 978-1-63228-031-2

Permissions:
"The Incredible Time Machine" from *In the Beak of a Duck* by Alan Gettis, Goodman Beck Publishing, 2008. Used by permission.

Library of Congress Cataloging-in-Publication Data is available.

To the policeman who gave me a speeding ticket; without him the idea for this book would not have happened.

CONTENTS

FOREWORD

Kristine Carlson

AS I READ through Allen Klein's book *You Can't Ruin My Day* I thought about how much my late husband, Dr. Richard Carlson, author of the *New York Times* best-selling series *Don't Sweat the Small Stuff,* would have appreciated the good humor and the essential wisdom of Klein's book.

A magical moment happened as I snuggled into my chair and began reading the introduction. A paragraph jumped out at me reminding me of a passage I had written in my journal from many years back.

Shortly after my husband's sudden departure (death) from a pulmonary embolism in 2006, I began to journal as part of my healing. In the beginning of this process of grieving, I couldn't type fast enough, and it seemed as though Richard was using my fingertips to speak to me through the keyboard. Here is something that appeared as a random thought one predawn morning in grief, as if Richard and I were sitting and having a conversation through the keyboard of my computer: "Enlightenment is far easier than anyone can imagine. It's not so much about what you do or don't do or how often you meditate or the position of your fingers as you do so. You quite simply have to just lighten up and stop taking life too seriously."

It was laughable, to me, that it was stated so simply.

Reading a similar passage in *You Can't Ruin My Day*, brought me a smile too. Allen says, "I mean, after all, who says that the road to enlightenment need be super serious? Even the word itself, 'enlightenment,' contains the word 'light.' In addition, many spiritual leaders know the value of humor and are lighthearted in their approach to life and learning."

This is so poignant and so true. (Thanks, Allen, for making me smile!)

I love the humor of Zig Ziglar, who said, "People say that motivation doesn't last. Well, neither does bathing. That's why we recommend it daily."

We all need to stay inspired to live life awake! *You Can't Ruin My Day* will provide you the daily motivation you need in order to live a happier, more inspired life.

Life is like a sport. You have to practice it the way you want to live it. And happiness is not a pursuit, but it is a perspective.

You Can't Ruin My Day is funny, lighthearted, and *real*, providing anecdotal advice that will help you gain the happiness perspective and mental dynamics you need—no matter what small annoyances come your way. Life is not just about getting through the big things that happen; it is even more about how you are able to manage the small stuff that can bring you down in a big way. Our lives are comprised of moments, hours, and days, and time flies fast into weeks, months, and years. If this were your last day on earth, you might not take those small things that happen so seriously—would you?

Allen shows us through his "Weekly Wake-Up Calls" that one of the wisest tools we have is the simple realization that there are pivotal moments, which are forks in the road, when you can gain perspective. While at this fork in the road, you get to decide if an incident or circumstance will alter your mood or not—thus, altering your day or not. There's a mindset that you can adopt where you learn to listen and hear the calls to action—those wake-up calls that can be a jingle or a nod to help navigate you on your way to greater peace and contentment.

Once we realize that we have a choice to be happy, it would be like banging your head against a wall to choose otherwise. Knowing this, why would you allow the minor annoyances in life to continue to upset you, or worse, ruin your day?

It boils down to the basic agreement you have with reality. Are you going to be victimized by life's circumstances or will you be a "victor" refusing to allow life's minor setbacks to disrupt your flow?

All of the annoyances, setbacks, and disappointments in life can all be wake-up calls and reminders to us of how incredible life is and that within the paradox of circumstances there is humor and wisdom and perfect order—as long as you listen and learn. Allen shows us that we have the power to label our experiences good or bad, positive or negative, helpful or hurtful. And, there is always a lesson to be learned and a blessing in those lessons. If you look back on your personal history, like dominoes in a row, I'm sure you can see how they all lined up to bring you where you are today.

I recently was on a media and speaking tour in Australia. I had packed way too much luggage, which I was carting around on a seven-city tour. I laughed, sometimes, as my arms and back hurt from lugging my bags up and down stairs. I thought to myself: Geez, Kris, how is this like your life? What kind of oversized baggage are you carrying around, and why are you doing that?

This book reminds me that I don't (metaphorically) have to carry my burdens like excess baggage. I can choose to travel more lightly. I can choose to literally lighten up!

Life can change on a dime, and every day matters.

You Can't Ruin My Day will help you shift gears into the most powerful choice you will ever make and that is to be victorious in your ability to choose an empowered approach to life. This book will wake you up and show you how this day may truly be the best day of your life—your speed bumps may slow you down just long enough for happiness to catch up to you.

Treasure the gifts of life and love.

Enjoy this book!

Kristine Carlson
Coauthor, with Dr. Richard Carlson, of the *Don't Sweat the Small Stuff* book series

START-UP

*Getting born is like being given a ticket to the
theatrical event called life. It's like going to the
theater. Now, all that ticket will get you is through the
door. It doesn't get you a good time and it doesn't get
you a bad time. You go in and sit down and you either
love the show or you don't. If you do, terrific. And if
you don't—that's show business.*

—STEWART EMERY,
self-help author and trainer

BACK STORY

I WAS DRIVING to the gym on a Saturday morning. I turned
up the music from the Broadway show *Billy Elliot* and sang
some of the lyrics about flying like a bird and being free.

That's when I heard a police siren. I was being pulled
over for speeding.

I had never had a speeding ticket before and I imagined that getting one would be a real bummer. But that was not the case. I knew it would cost me a bundle of money and a lot of time in traffic school, so I probably should have been really upset. But, instead, I had this incredible realization. No matter what happens to me, I realized that I have the power to control how it affects my day. I don't have to let anyone, or any situation, take that power away. I have total control over how I react to any given situation.

Yes, even to a speeding ticket.

On top of that, I also got a chuckle out of the incident. Being a senior citizen, and having never gotten a speeding ticket before, I thought to myself, "Gee, this is great, now I'm finally an adult!"

After getting the ticket, I got a wake-up call. I realized that I had the power to either let the ticket and policeman bring me down or I could continue my upbeat mood. By choosing the latter, as the song I was singing in the car reminded me, *I'm free, I'm free.*

I also realized that there are a lot of things I could do to help me stay up when the world is seemingly conspiring to bring me down. Thus came the idea for this book.

Writing is easy. All you do is sit staring at the blank sheet of paper until the drops of blood form on your forehead.

—GENE FOWLER,
journalist

FAST-FORWARD SEVERAL months after the speeding ticket incident. I bought, and now wear, a hearing aid. Whenever the battery is about to go out, a bell sound rings several times to the tune of Beethoven's *Fifth Symphony*..."Da-Da-Da-Dadah." It is a reminder that the battery needs changing.

This book is like the battery that is losing its power. It is a wake-up call to remind you that you need to change your mood whenever you are upset or angry. It is a reminder too that you have a choice. You can go on not hearing the joy that abounds in the world, or you can get a new battery to recharge and change your life.

Before we begin to explore ways to do that, let's take a quick look at what is in the book and how best to use it.

You Can't Ruin My Day contains fifty-two themes, or "Wake-Up Calls," as I've named them, to enhance your life by taking back your power and not letting other people or other situations ruin your day. It is organized into seven sections. They are:

Opening: START-UP
Part One: WAKE-UP
Part Two: WISE-UP
Part Three: GROW-UP (NOT!)
Part Four: CRACK-UP
Part Five: WRAP-UP
Closing: WIND-UP

Each of the 52 weekly themes contains three nuggets to chew on: Wake-Up Call—concepts about how to counteract the things that dampen your day; Follow-Up—practical things to implement the Wake-Up Call; and Lighten-Up—a lighthearted look related to the Wake-Up Call.

I invite you to try on each Wake-Up Call. See how it fits. See if you can take it and embrace it. If it doesn't fit after trying it for a while, then discard it and move on to the next one. If it works for you, keep it in your arsenal of things to help you maneuver around roadblocks, setbacks, or upsets that you might encounter on any given day.

While the Wake-Up Calls are under several different sections, they are really in no particular order in which you need to read them. You could follow them as they are written or you could pick out one from the table of contents and start there. Or maybe you'd like to open the book anywhere and start from there. What you need to know will find you in the perfect order that you need to know it.

It doesn't matter where you start. What matters is that you start getting your weekly wake-up booster shots. They are here to remind you not to give your power away to anyone or any circumstance. They are here to help you have a great day every day. They are here to reinforce the idea that no one or no event can ruin your day.

Be as playful as you want with the information in this book. No one says that the road to enlightenment need be serious. That's why I've included a Lighten-Up reminder in each Wake-Up Call. So don't skip over it. I mean, after all, who says that the road to enlightenment need be super serious? Even the word itself, "enlightenment," contains the word "light." In addition, many spiritual leaders know the value of humor and are lighthearted in their approach to life and learning.

One other thing...the word or short phrase title of each Wake-Up Call can be used as the word or phrase of the day to help you remember the lesson. Put it on a note above your computer. Hang it on your refrigerator with a magnet. However you choose to remember it, make it your saying for a period of time.

For me, the annoyances, setbacks, and disappointments in my life can all be wake-up calls, which remind me, in spite of it all, about how incredible life is and how perfect our world is. We are, after all, the ones who label our experiences good or bad, positive or negative, helpful or hurtful.

And, often, what appears to be not-such-a-great-thing at the time turns out to be either a blessing in disguise or a major teaching lesson.

For example, just recently my cousin used the phrase "a blessing in disguise" while telling me that she was fired from her job. Although she did not like her work or her boss, she continued to put up with her dissatisfaction for almost five years. Being fired was a wake-up call that showed her just how heavy the burden was she had been carrying around.

You Can't Ruin My Day is designed to help you unload the burdens you may have been carrying around with you. It is therefore not only filled with wise words but also with inspiring stories and anecdotes, insightful and motivational quotations, and lighthearted and laugh-producing material. In other words, this book is designed to help you put healthier, happier habits in motion for your personal growth.

The ability to see our lives as stories and share those stories with others is at the core of what it means to be human.

—JOHN CAPECCI AND TIMOTHY CAGE, *communication trainers*

I HAVE HAD some major losses in my life, including the death of my wife when she was thirty-four. All those losses have taught me that not only does life go on but that those setbacks can be my greatest teachers. I learned that what seemed like a devastating blow to my soul, in retrospect, deepened my growth and spirituality. What I also learned, and what I continue to learn, is that I can rise above any situation; that I don't have to let my circumstances rob me of my joyous spirit; that it will eventually be all right; and that I can take back my power and not let any person or any thing ruin my day, or, for that matter, my life.

When I was seven years old, my parents took me to see two Broadway musicals, *Carousel* and *Oklahoma*. From that day on I wanted to be the person who created "the pretty stage pictures." I wanted to be a scenic designer.

In grade school, I took shoeboxes and depicted a scene

from the book that the class was reading. Other students wrote book reports; I did dioramas. In high school, I saw almost every Broadway show, including the opening night of *Hello Dolly.* In college, I designed many of the school productions and, with the help of one of the professors, got into Yale Drama School. It was a three-year master's degree program. They admitted twelve students the first year. Then, because they only produced eight plays in their smaller theater the second year, they let go of four designers. I was one of the first to go. I was told I had no talent.

Soon after being booted from Yale, I became an apprentice in the scenic design union in New York City and finally became a full-fledged designer at CBS Television. My fellow classmates at Yale were still designing school productions while I was designing national television shows such as *Captain Kangaroo, The Merv Griffin Show,* and *The Jackie Gleason Show.*

Who said I had no talent? Who said I would never be a scenic designer? Nobody was going to ruin my day or my dream. Not even the head of the Yale School of Drama scenic design department!

More recently, that lesson was presented to me again. I guess sometimes we need reminders of things we've previously learned but need to hear again. So, my new mantra whenever not-so-wonderful stuff happens is: "Nobody can ruin my day. Nobody can ruin my day. Nobody can ruin my day."

I wanted a perfect ending. Now I've learned, the hard way, that some poems don't rhyme, and some stories don't have a clear beginning, middle, and end. Life is about not knowing, having to change, taking the moment and making the best of it, without knowing what's going to happen next.

—GILDA RADNER,
comedian

MATT WEINSTEIN, WHO is a friend and colleague, along with his wife Geneen Roth, who is an author and workshop leader, lost nearly all of their money in the Bernie Madoff scandal. It was a devastating blow robbing them of nearly a million dollars. Roth, a bestselling author and seminar leader, and Weinstein, a popular keynote speaker, were understandably shaken and shocked by the experience.

One minute all was well, and the next minute, with news delivered by a phone call, their world was shattered. What is so amazing, and what Roth writes about so elegantly in her book, *Lost and Found*, is that they did not let their loss ruin their lives.

"Although I never would have chosen the path of losing

our life savings," she says, "No matter what Bernard Madoff had stolen, no matter what I had lost or what I had left, I could only suffer to the degree that I allowed myself to fly off the ragged cliffs of my mind." And what Roth ultimately learned is what her spiritual teacher told her from the very beginning, "I promise you that nothing of any value is lost."

In spite of having thirty years of savings go down the drain in an instant, Roth noted that she "could still breathe. In this moment I could still see. In this moment there were still trees and wind and ground and birds. I had legs and arms and," she says jokingly, "chocolate."

After the initial shock of their setback, what Weinstein and Roth both realized is exactly what I'm talking about in this book—that absolutely no one, not even Bernard Madoff, could ruin their day. As Weinstein wisely notes in one of his talks, discontent comes from the stories we write for ourselves: "Yes, Bernie Madoff stole our money, but it was up to us to make sure he didn't steal the rest of our lives."

Matt Weinstein and Geneen Roth could have let their loss get in the way of them getting on with their life together. But they knew that resentment gets in the way of moving forward, that it would hold them back. They also knew that continually directing their anger and rage at Madoff would be a detriment to pursuing their careers. Instead, they chose not to feed into that, to focus on the future instead of the past, and to write their own story.

We're all stories, in the end.

—STEVEN MOFFAT,
TV writer and producer

I WAS AT a cocktail party recently talking with another author. He asked me what I was writing. When I told him, *You Can't Ruin My Day*, he started to laugh and asked, "Why can't someone ruin your day?"

I didn't have an immediate response at the time but when I thought about it later I realized that the answer is "because I won't let them." And that is the essence of this book—there are simple but profound ways to not let anyone or anything ruin your day.

So now it is your turn to write your own story. Start your journey and embrace the following fifty-two Wake-Up Calls to take back your power and change your life.

PART ONE

WAKE-UP

That is the real spiritual awakening, when something emerges from within you that is deeper than who you thought you were. So, the person is still there, but one could almost say that something more powerful shines through the person.

—ECKHART TOLLE,
author and spiritual teacher

CHANGE THE CHANNEL

⌘

*I think of life itself now as a wonderful play that I've
written for myself...and so my purpose is to have the
utmost fun playing my part.*

—SHIRLEY MACLAINE,
actress

O.K., SO SOMEBODY cut you off on the highway today.
You had a choice. You could have gotten really mad at them;
you could have cursed and raised your blood pressure to an
unhealthy level, or you could have calmed down and recal-
culated the situation.

Just like your GPS (Global Positioning System) gets you
moving in the right direction after you have made a wrong
turn, you can get back on track again by rewriting the script.

No, I'm not talking about the part where the driver cut you off, I'm talking about the part where you reacted to the situation—where you cursed and carried on about how rude drivers are, how no one pays attention to other people these days, how everyone is out to ruin your day. You could have changed the channel and changed your story with your own custom-made GPS. I'm talking about how to _Get a _Perspective _Shift by changing the channel.

Timothy Wilson, a psychologist at the University of Virginia, has been studying how small changes in a person's own story can change their life. He found that tiny tweaks in the interpretation of a life event could reap big benefits. He calls the process "story editing."

Wilson discovered that a revised story helped college students who were struggling academically. He found that if students told themselves "I'm bad at school," it led to a self-defeating cycle that kept them struggling. But if they told themselves a new story like "Everyone fails at first," they improved their grades and stayed in college.

Several years ago, I saw a wonderful play, _Clybourne Park_, in which the first act takes place in 1959 and the second act in 2009. One of the remarkable things about the play is that the same actors in the first act reappear fifty years later, most of them playing different characters. Here were the same actors we just saw and believed in act one playing totally different people in act two. And yet they were incredibly believable again.

Actors take on a role and convince us that they are

someone else. Good actors walk, talk, and think like the person they are portraying in spite of the fact that the words they are saying are not theirs. A scriptwriter has written it all for them.

Like actors, on some level we create our own worlds. Often, too, we think that everything revolves around us. Songwriter Carly Simon wrote about this in her song, "You're So Vain," in which she sings about someone who probably thinks the song is all about them. In reality, it may not be.

As another example, imagine that you are in a buffet restaurant and you accidently drop your dessert plate. Just as that happens, you notice a couple at a nearby table giving you nasty looks. Those disapproving looks remain in your mind all afternoon and end up ruining your evening. The truth of the matter is that the couple didn't even see you drop the plate. They were reacting to something one of them said to the other. They, in fact, hardly even know you existed, yet your mind created an entirely different scenario.

You may not be an experienced actor, or a scriptwriter, but you can still write your own story this week in your imagination and create the leading character, as you would like it to be. If you are fearful, act as if you are not. If you are mad at someone, make believe that you are best friends. If you are having a rotten day, make believe this is the best day of your life. Actors do it all the time. You can too.

Follow-Up

*It's taken me a long time to realize that when
someone is stuck they may really be more attached to
their story about being stuck than to any desire
to get unstuck.*

—JERRY GILLIES,
author

Years ago, I took the est Training founded by Werner Erhard. One of the things they taught and printed in the little booklet they gave out after the training was: "Obviously the truth is what's so. Not so obviously, it's also so what."

So you had a difficult childhood. So your parents yelled at you. So you lost your job. So you dented the car. So you have a nasty boss. So you didn't get the job you wanted. So your parents were divorced. So your flight was cancelled. So your partner left you. So... Some of these things may have happened a long time ago, some only a few hours ago. It doesn't matter. What matters is that you have the power to stop carrying these incidents around with you by retelling them in a different way.

This simple process of story editing works because, according to Wilson, trying to understand why a painful event happened is mentally consuming. People get stuck in thinking, "Why did he leave me?" or "Why was she so disappointed in me?" Subtle reframing changes that and helps us release those feelings.

On spiritualityhealth.com, yoga teacher Will Donnelly, who had his life partner of eleven years die of Lou Gehrig's disease (ALS), shares how the loss defined him and how he managed to change that:

"I heard myself telling the same story that I had shared with so many others since my partner died. To be fair, it was a true story, a heart-wrenching and bitter one. But it seemed that every time I shared it, instead of it helping me process the ordeal, it just reinforced the misery of it all. The story took me deeper into victimization each time I described it.

"I realized that I had begun to define myself by my struggle, and with each recount of the story, it echoed in my head for days, which felt terrible. In fact, my resentment began to wear me down; grief-fatigue overwhelmed me. It frightened me to know I would not be able to go on if the pain did not cease.

"The story, or, more importantly, *how I told the story*, had to change...

"Today, I consciously focus on the parts of the story that remind me of how resilient I am, how much I have been given in life, and how important love is. From this perspective, I now see life as such a remarkable and rich experience."

Remember that our lives unfold in the stories we tell ourselves. What story are you hanging on to and telling yourself today?

Lighten-Up

In her blog, *Tiny Buddha*, psychotherapist Rachel Whalley writes:

"Someone cuts you off in traffic. *What a jerk!* A date stands you up. *She obviously doesn't like you.* Your colleague gives you a dirty look across the room. *Your last email must have really pissed him off*!

Here's how I work with my own brain to stop getting so upset by all these little situations. I call it "Alternate Stories." Every time something happens that starts to get me feeling negative, judgmental, sad, or angry, I tell myself an alternate story about what might've been going on for the other person.

For example, say a person cuts me off in traffic.

My first response is to think, "Hey, look out, jerk!" And then I could proceed to get mad, feel my adrenaline rise, and start tailgating that car, just to show him he can't treat me like that.

But before I take any action or speak, I think to myself, "Is there any other possible reason that guy could have made that lane change right in front of me?"

Maybe he's on the phone hearing news that someone in his family just had to go to the hospital and is totally not paying attention.

Maybe *he's* trying to get to the hospital because he's having chest pains.

Maybe he's had a horrible day and his wife left him and

7

he's totally disconnected from anything besides his own pain.

Maybe he's just had a bug fly into his eye.

Maybe he really looked in his mirror and thought he saw no one there.

Maybe he's really nervous on the freeway and just made a mistake.

Or maybe he really is a jerk."

CHOOSE THE RIGHT CHANNEL

⌘

Others can shake you, surprise you, disappoint you, but they can't prevent you from acting, from taking the situation you're presented with and moving on. No matter where you are in life, no matter what your situation, you can always do something. You always have a choice and the choice can be power.

—BLAINE LEE,
author/businessman

IN THE 1994 popular film *Forrest Gump*, a bumper sticker salesman running alongside Forrest points out that he has just stepped in a pile of dog droppings. When Forrest replies, "It happens," the man replies, "What, sh*t?" To which Forrest responds, "Sometimes." The man is then inspired to create the "Sh*t Happens" bumper sticker.

And, indeed, "it" does happen. There is no avoiding it. Life is filled with imperfections and unforeseeable events. And when they or other annoying and distressing things occur, you assign a meaning to them. Yes, you, and only you, give a weight to any situation. You determine the importance of everything in your life.

Things are the way they are—like the changing seasons, or a loved one's dying, or rude, inconsiderate people. There are things in this world you can't control. What you can control, however, is how you react to those things. And it is the choices you make about those things that determine what kind of day, and life, you will have.

If you only get one thing out of this book, I hope it is: "There is no inherent meaning in any thought or action. You assign a meaning to everything."

And if there is one word behind every thought in this book, it is the word "choice," because that is really what this book is about. You either choose to let someone else, or something else, ruin your day, or you use the power that you have and choose to not let that happen.

Life is filled with choices. I have read that every day we make between forty thousand to sixty thousand choices: Do you want vanilla or chocolate ice cream?...Mustard or mayo on your sandwich?...An aisle or a window seat on the plane?... Take the highway or a local road?...Wear the red dress or the blue one?...A tie or none?...Leaded or unleaded gas?

Sometimes the choices are overwhelming. I often shop

at a large Chinese market in San Francisco. The shelf with soy sauce has more than a dozen brands and sizes from which to choose. And that is just for soy sauce. The store has hundreds of items like that.

Every millisecond of every day, you are making choices. But those choices are not only about physical things. Without even realizing it, every time you react to a situation, what you choose is also determining your emotional state as well.

Perhaps one of the most dramatic examples of someone using the power of choice to surmount their circumstance comes from psychiatrist and Holocaust survivor, Viktor Frankl. During his stay in a Nazi concentration camp, he, along with another prisoner, found something to laugh about every day. It gave him hope to look forward to the next day, and he credits it, in part, with his survival. "Everything can be taken from a man or a woman," says Frankl, "but one thing: the last of human freedoms to choose one's attitude in any given set of circumstances, to choose one's own way."

It is hard for me to imagine anything to laugh about while being incarcerated in a concentration camp. Yet, his extraordinary story addresses the issue of choice. No matter what our circumstance, we have the power to rise above it by the choices we make.

Perhaps you feel that you have been wronged by a family member, a friend, or a coworker. You may even feel justified in being angry with them, and you may be right. However, what you may not realize is that holding on to your anger or carrying a grudge against someone never serves you. It closes doors on relationships. It weighs you down and holds you back from moving forward. It zaps your energy—energy that you could use more productively to fully get pleasure from your relationships and enrich your life.

At my wedding reception, for example, I remember one cousin refusing to sit next to another cousin. Sometime in the past, they had had a disagreement. And the first cousin never forgot it. I had no idea that they weren't speaking to each other when I arranged for them to be at the same table. But that didn't matter. My first cousin bitched and moaned throughout the entire event about it. And, this fueled her complaining about almost everything else at the affair.

Did she have a good time at such a joyous occasion? No. Could she have had a good time? Yes, if she put the anger aside, chose to be happy, and enjoyed the other 149 people that were also in the room having a great time.

Opportunity Knocks

I grew up in New York City. So I never really needed a car, owned one, or learned to drive. When my wife and I moved to San Francisco, she was always the driver. After she died the car sat in the driveway for a long time. I would look at it every day and finally realized that I had a choice to make: I could sell the car; I could let it sit there and rust; or, I could learn to drive it.

I chose the latter. Little did I realize at the time but I could never do the work I was doing without knowing how to drive. Sometimes, for example, my travels took me to such remote places as Glasgow, Montana, or Wharton, Texas, or Farmington, Maine.

I could never have had a speaking career and spoken in all the out-of-the-way places around the country that I did if I didn't know how to drive. One door of my life had closed after my wife's death but another opened.

When things are not going well for you, when you are having a rotten day, remember that you have a choice. You could continually focus on those setbacks or see how they might be stepping-stones to something else.

Follow-Up

story is not your destiny. Who you were, what happened to you and all the struggles in your story do not have to determine who you will be. That is, unless you let it.

—MARY MANIN MORRISSEY,
spiritual teacher

Several months ago I was interviewed on a radio show. The host was pleased that I was her guest that day because she had just come from her daughter's house where there was a water main break that caused the basement to flood. The host was hoping that I could help her lighten up and not let it ruin her day.

To do this, I asked her if there was anything positive about the situation. She immediately listed two. First, she said that the water was clear and obviously not sewage. Second, she was glad that someone was in the house when it happened.

I assured her that she could probably find at least ten positive things about the water main break and that some of them might even be humorous. One might have been that for several hours it occupied her grandchild, who was home from school today; another that she would save money on watering the lawn; or even that she got to meet a new neighbor.

What stressful thing has happened to you this week? Are you assigning a negative label to it? Can you find at least five positive things about the situation?

Remember, there are hundreds of channels on TV, just as there are hundreds of possibilities for how you react to a situation. The channel you choose will determine how your day goes. Choose wisely.

Lighten-Up

A cowboy walks into a saloon. The bartender asks, "Care for a drink, stranger?"

The stranger asks, "What are my choices?"

And the bartender answers, "Yes or no!"

CURSE OR EMBRACE?

⌘

Your life is the sum result of all the choices you make,
both consciously and unconsciously. If you can
control the process of choosing, you can take control
of all aspects of your life. You can find the freedom
that comes from being in charge of yourself.

—ROBERT FOSTER BENNETT,
former U.S. senator

"YEARS AGO," SAYS therapist Dave Cooperberg, "I commuted across the San Francisco Bay Bridge. Driving home one evening I was feeling tired but relaxed after a good, hard day at work. Suddenly a driver decided to move from the fourth lane to the first, without bothering to use his indicator or consider the cars between him and where he went. I quickly braked, and felt the adrenaline shoot into my system as I went quickly from fear to anger. I told myself, 'This idiot could have killed me!' when I became aware—perhaps because my car was getting harder to control as I drove faster—that the peaceful mood I had was gone. Then a thought occurred to me: 'Why should I let this person's actions ruin my evening?' So I slowed down my driving and my breath. I made the conscious choice to let go of my outrage, no matter how righteous. I breathed out those feelings and returned to a state of peace, suddenly in awe of the power in making that choice."

Sometimes it may seem that the entire world is conspiring against you. It probably isn't but it still feels that way. In her lighthearted book about dealing with a loss, *Why Are the Casseroles Always Tuna?*, author and grief counselor Darcie Sims, has a perfect example of this. She writes:

"The whole world was picking on me today. Every single traffic light in the entire world was red, just for me, today! Everybody else had a green light, but not me. Oh, no! I got 281 red lights today! Not even a yellow, caution light—just red ones. Just for me.

"The faucet dripped all night, too. I was the only one who heard it, but it dripped all night! Just for me. They ran out of creamed broccoli on toast points at my favorite restaurant, and the mailman had mail for everyone in the house, except me!

"I got three hang-up phone calls on the answering machine and one I wished had hung up. My shoelace broke at the two-mile marker, and I had to walk home. Since I had forgotten my key, I had to wait for my four-mile husband to come back. I sat on the curb and waited and got two mosquito bites...."

So, what do you do when it feels like the world is out to get you? Hitting your head on the wall hurts. Hitting someone could get you locked up. Hitting the bottle could result in a major hangover.

Of course, getting away from it all by taking a nap might help, but that is not usually possible, especially if you are at work. Taking a long walk might also help to clear your head, but that may not be possible either. One thing you can do, that will work, is to embrace your situation instead of cursing it.

Phil Hansen is someone who has done that. In art school he developed a tremor in his hand that prevented him from creating the pointillism drawings he loved. For three years he gave up art until a neurologist suggested that instead of letting his condition stop him from producing works of art, he could "embrace the shake."

With this new way of looking at his setback, what started out as something that limited him actually liberated him. When his funds were too small to purchase art supplies, he made art from coffee cups. When he couldn't afford canvas, he used his body on which to paint. At other times, instead of using his hands to create his artwork, he used his mouth or his feet. What was originally limiting became limitless.

Arnold Beisser, a former national tennis champion, contracted polio at age twenty-four and was confined to an iron lung. Instead of lamenting his situation he celebrated it. Lying on his back and staring at the ceiling most of the time, he says:

"Eventually, I could pass a very interesting time looking at the ceiling, noticing small details and changes.... I played with the sounds I heard, listening now to the voice tones of a speaker, and then to the words, then perhaps shifting to some background noise, in the room. Instead of looking only at people's eyes, I noticed noses, and ears, and mouth expressions, and skin color. I began to see others in ways I had not seen before, in richer ways.... Sometimes, if I were lucky, I would become like a child and perceive the world like an ever-changing kaleidoscope picture."

If Beisser, who spent a good part of his life in an iron lung, could see the world as a colorful kaleidoscope in spite of his debilitating circumstance, and if Hansen could "embrace the shake," then you too can embrace your trying situation instead of focusing on the irritation and upset.

After my wife died at the age of thirty-four from a rare liver disease, I thought my life was over. I had never experienced such a major loss before and could not see how I would go on without her. One of the things that helped me cope was focusing on what was right about my life rather than on what wasn't. Knowing that I still had my ten-year-old daughter helped me survive the loss. I also had my health, a roof over my head, and a profitable business.

Sure you may be going through a difficult phase in your life right now. Sure you may feel despondent about what is happening. Sure you may feel that everything is going wrong. But that doesn't negate all the positive things in your life.

Part of the key to getting through the difficulty you might be having is to focus on what is right with your life instead of what is wrong. That way you can make a lousy day into a lovely one.

~~~~~~~~~~~~~~~~~~~~~~~~~~~~~

Bummer or Bump in the Road?

One day a woman in a nursing home raised her fist in the air and shouted across the large meeting hall, "Tonight I will have sex with any man who can tell me what I'm holding in my hand right now."

A man across the room yells out, "An elephant."

The woman replies, "Close enough. You won!"

At the beginning of any joke, you are given a story, a statement, or a question. At some point in the joke, what you were presented with at the start turns into something that you didn't expect. You feel duped or surprised and so you laugh.

In the joke above, what started out one way turns into another. At the beginning of the joke, we don't know where it will take us, and by the end of the joke, we don't expect it to conclude as it does.

Life is like the structure of a joke. First something happens. Life throws you a punch—you go along and suddenly somebody does something that angers you, or, perhaps, you accidentally lock your keys in the car. Then, just like the punch line of a joke, you can take whatever irritating thing that has happened and turn it around, get a new perspective, and see it in a more positive way.

Dan Burris, business strategist, flies a lot for his company and hence frequently encounters delays, cancellations, and travel problems. He notes, "Someone sitting next to me [on a plane] asked if I still like flying after logging many millions of miles in the air. I would say yes, because flying enables me to help people all over the world, people I would never see or meet if I could not cover a lot of ground fast and to me that's one of the great blessings of flying. Sure delayed flights can at first feel like a bummer, but in the bigger picture of life, it's really just a small inconvenience."

Burris asks, "Is the problem or 'bummer' you are currently facing really just an inconvenience compared to what other people with real problems might be facing?"

Follow-Up

Try not to take things so personally. After all, if you are going to say "Why me?" when you experience frustration, disappointment, and challenges, then you might as well say, "Why me?" when you experience love, kindness, friendship, and joy.

—ALAN GETTIS,
psychologist

One of the things you can do this week when something upsets you is, like the punch line of a joke, turn that annoyance around and get a different view of the situation. Every time you think that something, or someone, is attacking you, realize that you have the power to either get caught up in its dark side or steer your thoughts toward the sunny side of the street.

Ask yourself: "Do I want to be right or do I want to be happy?" If your answer is "I want to be happy," then: Choose peace over an upset. Choose to be grateful. Choose to forgive. Choose to make happiness a priority. Choose to embrace the situation instead of cursing it.

Lighten-Up

I used to live near one of the steepest hills in San Francisco. One day I noticed a sign at the top of the incline. Someone crossed out "Steep Hill" and wrote "Cliff."

ACCEPT THINGS AS THEY ARE

⌘

We must learn to accept.... To accept life, and to accept ourselves, not blindly and not with conceit, but with a shrug and a smile. To accept in the end existence, not because it's just or reasonable or even satisfactory, but simply and plainly because it's all we've got.

—HARVEY MINDESS,
psychologist

LATER IN HIS life, the Indian philosopher J. Krishnamurti surprised his audience at a lecture by asking, "Do you want to know my secret?" Those who had been following the teachings of the spiritual leader for years were excited to hear his answer and finally learn the key to understanding.

"This is my secret," he said. "I don't mind what happens."

Until you accept things the way they are, and realize that you can't change other people, except perhaps by setting an example of how you would like them to be, you will be hard-pressed to find a lot of happiness in your day.

Until you are content with where you are, or whatever situation you are in, you will never be happy if you want situations to be other than they are. As Eckhart Tolle, author of *The Power of Now*, reminds us, "Stress is caused by being 'here' but wanting to be 'there,' or being in the present but wanting to be in the future."

If, for example, you wanted to go to Paris for years, and your plane lands in Rome because all the airline personnel in Paris are on strike, and it doesn't look like you will get to Paris at all, you may be extremely disappointed. But, if you let go of your attachment to Paris and enjoy the incredible beauties of Rome, you can still have a wonderful time. And who knows, maybe even a better time than you might have had in Paris, especially if you meet some wealthy irresistible Roman.

Commenting on accepting what is, spiritual teacher and author Louise L. Hay says, "When we do not flow freely with life in the present moment, it usually means we are holding on to a past moment. It can be regret, sadness, hurt, fear, or guilt, blame, anger, resentment, and sometimes even the desire for revenge. Each one of these states comes from a space of unforgiveness, a refusal to let go and come into the present moment."

In the Academy Award–nominated documentary,

Complaints of a Dutiful Daughter, Deborah Hoffmann explores her mother's struggle with Alzheimer's disease. At first, Hoffmann is expectedly upset that, among other things, her mother no longer recognizes her. But, once Hoffmann accepts her mother's condition and gets into her mother's frame of mind, they can begin to relate and enjoy each other once again. In fact, Hoffmann acknowledges that once she was able to accept her mother's condition, she could more easily find some humor in the situation.

What difference does it make if the mother thinks that it's June when in reality it's August? Or, that the mother thinks both of them went to high school together? What does make a big difference in their relationship is Hoffmann's acceptance of the situation.

The same is true of some of the difficulties you might be facing right now. Chances are they are difficult because you are not accepting them as they are. You are trying to change them to fit your viewpoint. You may not agree with how your boss is handling a client, or how a coworker is doing their job, or whom your daughter is dating. You can express your opinion about it but if they don't change, you are only causing yourself undue stress and unhappiness continually trying to change them. To avoid them ruining your day, you need to accept the situation and move on.

Hoffmann could not change the fact that her mother had Alzheimer's disease. What she could do, and did, was to accept her mother as she was and, knowing that, change the way she related to her.

26

~~~~~~~~~~~~~~~~~~~~~~~~~~~~~~~~

Ride the Horse in the Direction It's Going

In *The Seven Whispers*, author Christina Baldwin writes, "I long ago discovered that the only way to stop a runaway horse is by first calming myself and then calming the animal. No amount of screaming helps. No amount of pleading. No amount of waiting for instructions from the roadside. The horse will run until it has run itself out, or I will find a way to slow the momentum and come back into relationship with what I am riding: becoming two beings moving with one gait."

One major key to not letting something ruin your day is to take control by accepting what is. Or, as est founder, Werner Erhard, playfully reminds us, "It's much easier to ride the horse in the direction he's going."

If you had a horse, for example, and you wanted to go in one direction and the horse wanted to go in another, sorry folks, but it isn't going to work. No amount of pulling or tugging, kicking or screaming, pleading or prodding will make the horse go where you want it to go if the horse doesn't want to go there. And, don't forget, he is much bigger than you. So accepting the place where the horse is headed is easier.

To be content, and have a great day every day, you need to accept other people and situations as they are, not the way you want them to be. I'm not saying *not* to try to make the world better. But it is useless to keep knocking your head against the wall trying to change things that can't be changed.

A friend of mine who lives in New Jersey, author and spiritual teacher John Welshons, has a great example of acceptance. One time he journeyed to Maui, Hawaii, for a couple of weeks. On his return home, it was an incredibly magnificent day in the Islands; the sun was shining, the breeze was delightfully coming off the ocean, and the aqua-colored water was crystal clear. When he got off the plane in Newark, it was cloudy, damp, and foggy. Sure he would have preferred to be back in Maui enjoying the beautiful sunshine. But he wasn't. He was in New Jersey. And, he realized that if he were attached to being in Maui, he would never be happy no matter where he was.

Certainly we can have preferences. But we are in big trouble when we get attached to them.

~~~~~~~~~~~~~~~~~

Follow-Up

Acceptance doesn't mean resignation; it means understanding that something is what it is and that there's got to be a way through it.

—MICHAEL J. FOX,
actor

Last Christmas, I received a box of Harry & David pears. If you have never had these, they are the ultimate of what a pear should be—big, juicy, and near perfect. I say near perfect because a couple of pears had small bruises on them—nothing serious, and nothing that would affect the flavor, but still not absolutely perfect.

Life, I realized, is like those pears. Things can be near perfect. Nothing very serious is happening yet we complain about some small annoyance or get bent out of shape if someone ticks us off. But we needn't let it if we can just accept what life is, with all its imperfections.

Before you get upset and let someone or something ruin your day, stop and ask yourself: "Am I willing to allow things to be just as they are?"

To help you accept the world as it is, below is an abbreviated version of an "Accepting Reality Exercise" that I found on the Internet:

Sit with yourself in silent meditation and visualize something that you have a hard time accepting. It could be a person, a situation, a health problem, or simply just a part of you in your mind's eye.

Imagine embracing the situation. Imagine all the resistance, struggle, judgments, and expectations you feel toward this situation just melting and releasing away. Say to it (out loud or to yourself): *"I accept you just as you are."*

Trust that this situation is just what you need. Trust that this situation is leading you to something bigger that you may not understand right now. Trust and surrender.

In Buddhist thinking, suffering comes from nonacceptance. When you let go of the way you *think* things should be and stop resisting the way things are, when you accept what is and stop pushing away things you don't want and embrace what you have, your life will dramatically change for the better.

Lighten-Up

Once, when humorist Robert Benchley was leaving a Manhattan nightclub, he turned to the man in uniform at the door and said, "Would you please get us a taxi?"

The man replied, "I'm sorry, sir, but I happen to be a Rear Admiral in the United States Navy."

"All right, then," Benchley responded, "get us a battleship."

LEARN TO LET GO

⌘

*You will find that it is necessary to let things go,
simply for the reason that they are heavy. So let them
go, let go of them. I tie no weights to my ankle.*

—C. JOYBELL C.,
author

IT HAD BEEN an incredibly frustrating morning. When I got to my desk, I discovered that my credit card company had emailed me that there had been an attempted fraudulent charge to my account. I immediately called them. Because of what happened, they wanted to cancel my account and issue me a new card. I didn't want that. (I had a similar experience the previous year and it took a lot of time to contact the merchants who automatically deduct their payments from my account. And for several merchants, who only bill me once or twice a year, I forgot that they were on an automatic schedule so when the bill came through it never got paid.)

After the first person refused to let me keep my card, I spent about forty minutes on hold, waiting to speak to a supervisor. I finally made a deal with them to keep the card but get a new one if a fraudulent charge happened again.

Then I attempted to stamp a letter that I had written the night before only to find that my stamp machine had a "lockout" message on it. Usually it is only a matter of minutes to clear the lockout, but every time I tried it didn't work. Finally, after several tries and more frustration, it cleared.

Just as I thought things were running smoothly again, my attempt to back up my computer didn't work either. Again, it took a number of tries and mounting frustration against technology that wasn't cooperating this morning.

On days like this, in an attempt to get a little levity in the situation, I often say, "The moon must be in tapioca." I have no idea where I got that phrase but it always brings a small smile to my face when I'm frustrated. But even better, I realized that I didn't have to let a bad beginning ruin my entire day when I read my Unity *Daily Word* publication.

The word of the day was "surrender." How very appropriate for what I was experiencing that morning. How appropriate anytime. "In the midst of disagreement," it said, "I may be tempted to give in to frustration. Yet, no matter what happens outside, I have the ability to choose how to respond."

Speaking about surrendering and letting go reminds me of an old Zen story about two monks who were walking down the road and noticed a woman waiting to cross a stream. To the dismay of one monk, the other went over to the woman, picked her up, and carried her across the water. About a mile down the road, the monk who was aghast at his friend's action remarked, "We are celibate, we are not supposed to even look at a woman, let alone pick one up and carry her across a stream. How could you possibly do that?"

The other monk turned and replied, "I put the woman down a mile back. Are you still carrying her around with you?"

Letting go of those things that irritate us is not easy. But not letting go can be even worse.

When we hold on to such states as anger, resentment, and rage, it becomes an overwhelming force. It dominates our thoughts, zaps our energy, and ruins our day. It prevents a lot of other, perhaps more positive, uplifting things from entering our life. That clutter is like a desk piled so high with papers that it prevents us from finding a place to work. Or like a stream that gets clogged with so many leaves, branches, and debris that the water can only trickle through. We have got to clear the debris of our mind, let it go, and let things flow again.

Not letting go is like the monkey who put his hand into an urn with a small opening. Panicking, the monkey clenched his fist and tried to pull his arm out. But it was impossible. His fist was too large for the small opening. The more he tried, the more frustrated and angry he became. Finally he gave up and relaxed his fist. As soon as he did, his hand easily slipped out of the urn.

Like the monkey, we too get trapped in our predicaments. But, like the lesson we can learn from the monkey, sometimes all we need to do to get out of our stuck place is to let go and stop struggling.

A friend of mine, Laura, has a powerful story of how letting go probably saved her life. One day, when she was nineteen years old, she was walking down the street when two men grabbed her and threw her into their car. They told her to cooperate or else they would kill her. They drove to a remote park where one of the men began to rape her. Laura was terrified and resisted with everything she had. As she started to fight off her attacker, he started to hit her.

"I wanted to live," says Laura. "I fought with everything I had." But the more she fought, the more her assailant struck her. At that moment, she says, "It felt like some part of me split off as I heard these words in my head, 'Stop fighting. Don't fight anymore.'"

Even though she thought it was a crazy idea, with those words, she went limp and calmness came over her. Suddenly she was addressing her attacker in a voice that had no fear. "It took me by surprise," she says. "I could feel his power and drive and force were lessened. And it wasn't long before he sat in the seat next to me because he couldn't continue the rape."

This is a powerful story of letting go of a physical

struggle. Laura also had many years of learning to let go of the psychological struggle after dealing with her traumatic experience. But she has done both and is now a wonderful human being in a profession helping others to let go of their life struggles.

We all have our past stories—some neutral, some good, and some not so good. When we continue to carry around those past events that have caused us pain, we can't fully experience our life now because they color everything we do. At some point, we need to let them go and move on with our life. Perhaps easier said than done, but nonetheless something we must do in order to not let those past events ruin our current circumstances.

Another example comes from a friend who experienced turbulence on the first flight he ever took. Since that time he will only travel by car or train, even on long trips. A plane ride would have taken only an hour or two. However, he may spend, say, eight hours to several days traveling because his past experience is influencing his life, perhaps forever.

You may not be afraid of turbulence or have as dramatic a story as Laura's. But we all have things in our past that continue to color our present and our future. We need to let go of those things, write a new story, and move on in order to have a richer, happier life.

~~~~~~~~~~~~~~~~~~~~~~~~~~~~~~~~

Create a Celebration Fund

"I had a boyfriend once who didn't love me. Usually I am so humiliated by the memory of how I threw myself at his feet that I either repress everything he ever said to me or else portray him in my books as heartless and ignorant....

"But this morning...I suddenly recalled something he said during a fight we had...'Why not think of all the times we've celebrated and all the times we have yet to celebrate as a bank account from which we can draw funds?' he asked. 'Let's take some celebration savings out now, put aside this fight, and replenish the fund when we get home.'

"I remember...thinking I could let this horrible fight go.... Then I thought, but if I let it go, I will be a wimp. He doesn't deserve to have a good time after what he's done...so I said, 'Forget it. It's a terrible idea,' and ruined the evening for us both.

"It has taken me thirteen years to remember that I was enchanted by the notion of a celebration fund, and to admit that even cads can have brilliant ideas.... Rather than focus on how fat and miserable we are, or how fabulous life will be when we change, we can put our attention on what is right in our lives right now. You'll be surprised at the sea change in your attitude. It's like taking off in an airplane during a rainstorm and flying above the clouds. You suddenly realize that the luminous blue has been there all the time."

—Geneen Roth,
author of *When You Eat at the Refrigerator,
Pull Up a Chair*

~~~~~~~~~~~~~~~~~~~~~~~~~~~~~~

Follow-Up

Even though you may want to move forward in your life, you may have one foot on the brakes. In order to be free, we must learn how to let go. Release the hurt. Release the fear. Refuse to entertain your old pain. The energy it takes to hang on to the past is holding you back from a new life. What is it you would let go of today?

—MARY MANIN MORRISSEY,
spiritual teacher

When we hear an MC introduce a comedian, they often ask the audience to "give it up" for the performer. They are referring to acknowledging enthusiasm for the performer and welcoming them to the stage. You might want to remember this phrase and give up whatever is getting in your way of having a sensational day.

Note what you struggle with this week. Then, with Laura's

courageous story in mind, or, like the monk on the road, give it up and get on with the show.

Lighten-Up

A carpenter had just finished a rough first day on the job. A flat tire made him lose an hour of work, his electric saw quit, and then his ancient pickup truck refused to start.

A fellow worker drove him home. On arriving, he invited his coworker in to meet his family. As the carpenter walked toward the front door, he paused briefly at a tall tree, touching the tips of the branches with both hands. When opening the door, he underwent an amazing transformation. His face had a big smile on it. He hugged his two small children and gave his wife a kiss.

Afterward he walked his coworker to the car, passing the tree that he touched earlier. When the coworker asked about the tree, the carpenter replied: "Oh, that's my trouble tree. I know I can't help having troubles on the job, but one thing's for sure—troubles don't belong in the house with my wife and the children. So I just hang them up on the tree every night when I come home. Then in the morning I pick them up again."

"Funny thing is," said the carpenter, "when I come out in the morning to pick 'em up, there ain't nearly as many as I remember hanging up the night before."

GET OUT OF THE WAY

⌘

A pessimist sees the difficulty in every opportunity;
an optimist sees the opportunity in every difficulty.

—WINSTON CHURCHILL,
British politician

SEVERAL YEARS AGO I adopted a beautiful Australian cattle dog mix from a rescue shelter. I enrolled her in dog training school and puppy socialization classes. In spite of that, she still did things that I didn't like. Being a puppy, I knew it would take a while for her to learn new behaviors. But I was impatient until a friend of mine, who has two dogs, reminded me: "She is a dog. You can train her all you want, but remember, she is still a dog."

It was also a good lesson about human beings too. You

can't change other people. I may not like what you do or how you behave, but I can't force you to change. I can be an example of how I would like you to behave or talk with you about things you do that irritate me, but in the long run, I can't change you.

My dad was a good example of that. He had a very negative outlook on life. For him, the glass was always half empty. He would constantly worry about what might go wrong instead of what might be right.

For over a month, before my parents took a cross-country train trip to visit me, he grumbled and worried about how his luggage might get lost in Chicago where they had to change trains. Every time I spoke to him on the telephone, he lamented about the luggage.

So, what do you think happened when my mom and dad changed trains? Of course, the luggage got lost. I'm not saying that he created this and I'm not saying that he didn't, but certainly his overwhelming and constant negative energy did not help with the joy and anticipation of planning a trip.

Most of my life, I was upset at his negativity until I realized that I could step back, let go, get out of the way, and simply watch his shenanigans instead of getting caught up in them. In fact, once I learned to do that, it helped me love him more, and not get so angry at him, and, once in a while, even smile or chuckle at his antics. This became really clear to me one day when I was helping my parents get settled in a new apartment.

They had lived all of their lives in New York and moved to a new condo in Florida. I flew there to help them unpack. For the entire time I was there, my dad complained that the baseboard outlets in their bedroom did not work.

I said, "Dad, you have a maintenance contract, why don't you just call them to come and fix it?"

He responded, "Because you never know when they will show up."

I said, "Yes, Dad, but you never leave the house. What difference does it make when they show up?"

He didn't reply, nor did he call them. All he did was complain that it wasn't working.

I started to get angry and then realized that I couldn't change him. I let go, got out of the way, and simply watched his antics. Then several days later, I got a good laugh.

The morning I was leaving to fly back home, I flipped the light switch on the wall in the bedroom. Suddenly several of the lamps went on indicting that the baseboard outlets worked!

~~~~~~~~~~~~~~~~~~~~~~~~~~~~

Let It Come to You

Have you ever had the experience of misplacing something, not finding it after a lot of searching, and then have it suddenly appear?

The same could be true about some of the

41

challenges you are, or will be, facing this week. Maybe you are searching too hard. Maybe you need to let go and let the resolution come to you.

A couple of years ago, after I got the rights back to several of my out-of-print books, I tried in vain to find a new publisher for them. For a year and a half, I struggled every day seeking a new publisher. Frustrated in not finding one, I gave up actively looking and put a sign above my desk that read: "The Perfect Publisher Will Find Me."

Then, one day, I went to a meeting of book publicists. I hadn't been to one of their meetings for years, but I wanted to hear the guest speaker that day. At the event, the man next to me was chatting with two women behind him. I overheard them say that they were starting a new division of their publishing company and that they were looking for books that uplift, inspire, and bring joy to readers. When I heard that, I immediately introduced myself and told them how well my out-of-print books would fit in their new division.

They gave me their card and asked that I send them my books. When I saw their address, I knew that I had found the perfect publisher. Their offices were only five blocks from where I live. So I hand-delivered my books the next day and the rest is history. They have since published eight of my books including this one.

And there is more to the story...shortly after I

signed my first contract with the publisher, they had a party to celebrate their new, larger offices. When I walked in the door, a woman approached me and said that she owned the company and that she was pleased that I was going to be one of their authors. Moreover, she said, "I know you." She told me that she now lived in London but for sixteen years she lived across the street from me and watched me walk my dog every day.

Indeed, the perfect publisher found me!

Follow-Up

By letting it go, it all gets done. The world is won by those who let it go. But when you try and try, the world is beyond the winning.

—LAO TZU,
Chinese philosopher

I have always felt that if I am struggling too hard to accomplish something, perhaps it is not supposed to happen, or at least not at that time. Sometimes all you have to do is to get out of the way and let it happen, let go, and let it come to you.

What are you struggling with right now?

What have you wanted that is not happening?

Can you let go of those things and let them come to you?

Maybe you want to have a sign near you each day this week that says, "The perfect _____ (fill in what you are seeking, i.e., a job, a partner, an apartment, etc.) will find me."

Lighten-Up

A man named Sam was walking along a steep cliff one day, when he accidentally got too close to the edge and fell. On the way down he grabbed a branch, which temporarily stopped his fall. He looked down and to his horror saw that the canyon plunged straight down for several hundred feet. He couldn't hang on much longer, so Sam began yelling for help, hoping that someone passing by would hear him and lower a rope to save him.

"Help! Help! Is anyone up there?"

He yelled for a long time, but no one heard him. He was about to give up when he heard a voice. "Sam. Sam. Can you hear me?"

"Yes, yes! I can hear you. I'm down here!"

"I can see you, Sam. Are you all right?"

"Yes, but who are you, and where are you?"

"I am God. I'm everywhere."

"God, please help me! I promise if you'll get me down

from here, I'll stop sinning. I'll be a really good person. I'll serve you for the rest of my life."

"Let's get you off from there; then we can talk."

"Now, here's what I want you to do. Listen carefully."

"I'll do anything, God. Just tell me what to do."

"O.K. Let go of the branch."

"What?"

"I said, let go of the branch. Just trust Me. Let go."

There was a long silence.

Finally Sam yelled, "Help! Help! Is anyone else up there?"

STOP PLAYING THE BLAME GAME

⌘

Take your life in your own hands, and what happens?
A terrible thing: no one to blame.

—ERICA JONG,
author

WHEN I WAS growing up, my parents took me to see the movie *Gilda* in which actress Rita Hayworth plays a "femme fatale" named Mame. She sings a somewhat sexy tongue-in-cheek song, "Put the Blame on Mame," in which she fictitiously takes credit for causing, among others, everything from the great Chicago fire to the 1906 San Francisco earthquake.

That movie and that song brought to mind how often we don't take responsibility for our discontent. We blame our spouse for things we don't like in the relationship. We blame our parents for not doing things we thought they should have done. We blame our boss for making unreasonable demands. We blame our teacher for giving us a bad grade. We blame our sibling for not treating us well. We blame the weather for ruining our picnic. We blame the airline for our cancelled flight. We blame the clerk for overcharging us. We blame God for not answering our prayers. We blame. We blame. We blame. The list is endless.

Some people in the news too have absurdly put the blame on things that could not have possibly caused them. Sometimes they are so outrageous that they are laughable. For example, one headline noted, "Pastor blames Colorado floods on abortion, weed, and 'decadent homosexual activity.'" In another news story, a man got stuck on train tracks and blamed it on his GPS. And, not long ago, one leading newscaster blamed the Internet for mass ignorance.

As discussed in a previous Wake-Up Call, by accepting things as they are, we can stop blaming others for our unhappiness. We can take responsibility and deal with things as they are. When we blame others for our discontent, we are copping out. When we blame others, we are focusing our energy away from us and neglecting the opportunity for our own growth and learning.

Spiritual leader Pema Chödrön has talked about why blame holds us back. Since she does it more elegantly than I can, I will let her expound on the subject: "We habitually erect a barrier called blame that keeps us from communicating

47

genuinely with others, and we fortify it with our concepts of who's right and who's wrong. We do that with the people who are closest to us and we do it with political systems, with all kinds of things that we don't like about our associates or our society. It is a common, ancient, well-perfected device for trying to feel better. Blame others.... Blaming is a way to protect your heart, trying to protect what is soft and open and tender in yourself. Rather than own that pain, we scramble to find some comfortable ground."

Take responsibility for your actions or the situation you may have caused. Don't make others your scapegoat. Stop saying things like, "You did this to me." "It's your fault that I..." "You started it all!" Take responsibility for your own life and your own happiness.

One other thing about blaming (which is the opposite of praise)—when you begin to find fault or judge someone else, you can simply substitute admiration. A very powerful example of this comes from a tribe in Africa. Instead of blaming someone who has done something hurtful, they shower him with praise. First that person is placed alone in the center of the village. Then every man, woman, and child gathers around them in a large circle. Each person, regardless of age, speaks out loud to the accused and tells them about all the good things that person has done in his lifetime.

Every good deed, attribute, kindness, and strength is carefully told in detail. The ceremony often lasts for days and doesn't end until every positive comment has been stated. At the end, the circle is broken, a celebration takes place, and the person is welcomed back into the tribe.

~~~~~~~~~~~~~~~~~~~~~~~~~~~

No More Cramps

In his wonderful book, *The Theft of the Spirit*, psychiatrist Carl Hammerschlag writes about an eighteen-year-old young man named Hugh, who was considered one of the best competitive rock climbers in the country. On one climbing expedition, Hugh was caught in a blizzard. Soaked, freezing, and nearly dead from both hypothermia and frostbite, he was finally rescued after spending two harrowing days in the wilderness. But both legs had to be amputated just below the knee.

Hugh could have blamed a lot of things for his loss—the poor weather conditions, the slow rescuers, the medical team that removed his legs, etc. But he didn't. "Within a year," Hammerschlag tells us, Hugh "learned to design and make himself new feet." And he also created "feet" for regular climbing as well as specific conditions, like ones for narrow crevices or ice climbing. He regained his ability to climb mountains and once more excelled in the sport.

Hugh also has a sense of humor about his loss. When asked by a reporter what it was like to climb now as opposed to before the accident, he said, "Now my calves don't cramp."

~~~~~~~~~~~~~~~~~~~~~~~~~~~

Follow-Up

We are taught you must blame your father, your sisters, your brothers, the teacher—but never blame yourself. It's never your fault. But it's always your fault, because if you wanted to change you're the one who has got to change.

—KATHARINE HEPBURN,
actress

My father was a printer all of his life. He loved being a printer and liked his job. But he disliked his bosses. Often he disagreed with the way they were handling a job and frequently he had to work overtime, particularly on Friday nights. At those times, he would come home tired and irritated. As a result, no matter what my mother made for dinner, he would often complain about it. In spite of her hard work making the meal, he would push it aside and only want melon and sour cream, one of the things he liked.

It would upset my mother and often yelling and tears would follow. He blamed my mom for making a lousy meal when in reality he was the one who had a lousy day. Looking back, I realize that he could not take his frustration out on his bosses, or he might lose his job, so he took it out on her.

Therapists have found that we often take our anger out on those closest to us, those we love the most. We say things to them we might never say to strangers. Perhaps it is because we are around them for longer periods of time than with others. Perhaps it is because we don't stop and think before we lash out. No matter the reason, if that happens this week, before you blame someone else, below are five possible things you might do before things escalate.

Put yourself in the other person's shoes. Ask yourself, "If I were them, how would I like to be treated?"

Stop. The moment you become angry or upset with someone, don't say anything. Instead, pause for a moment.

Walk away. If necessary, leave the scene.

Distract yourself. Look around and find something to take your mind off the situation.

Do something about it. It's natural to be angry, particularly about the injustices of the world. "If you're not angry," says poet Maya Angelou, "you are either a stone or you are too sick to be angry." But she says, "You must not be bitter. Bitterness is like cancer—it eats upon the host.... So use your anger. Yes, you write it, you paint it, you dance it, you march it, you vote it..."

Lighten-Up

One day a man goes into the lunchroom at work and sits down next to his friend. He opens his lunch bag and takes out a sandwich. He takes it out of the plastic baggie and exclaims, "Yuck!"

His friend asks, "What's the matter?"

The man says, "A cheese sandwich. I hate cheese sandwiches."

The next day he has lunch with the same friend. Opening his lunch bag, he proclaims, "Oh no, I can't believe it. Another cheese sandwich."

On the third day, the man has lunch with his friend and again he discovers a cheese sandwich.

Trying to comfort him, the man's friend says, "If you don't mind me asking, why don't you tell your wife to make you a different kind of sandwich?"

"Oh, I'm not married," the man replies.

"Well then, who makes your cheese sandwiches every day?" the friend asked.

"I do," replies the man.

FORGIVE OTHERS

⌘

When you hold resentment toward another, you are bound to that person or condition by an emotional link that is stronger than steel. Forgiveness is the only way to dissolve that link and get free.

—CATHERINE PONDER,
author

HARBORING HURTS AND grudges is detrimental to having a great day. One of the most powerful ways to counteract that is through forgiveness.

Several years ago I received a letter from a woman who read one of my books. She had been violently raped twice when she was twelve years old. She was now sixty-seven and she had never told anyone about the horrific incidents.

For years she was angry and full of rage until she read a quotation by Dale Carnegie in one of my books. The quotation was: "When we hate our enemies, we are giving them power over us: power over our sleep, our appetites, our blood pressure, our health, and our happiness. Our enemies would dance with joy if only they knew how they were worrying us, lacerating us, and getting even with us! Our hate is not hurting them at all, but our hate is turning our days and nights into a hellish turmoil."

After reading it, the woman said that the words impacted her in a profound way. It gave her courage and enabled her to forgive her abductor. "I've taken my power back," she wrote, "and it has changed my life."

Last year, there was a powerful story of forgiveness on the evening news. It was about Mary Johnson whose only son was shot to death during an argument at a party. The murderer was a sixteen-year-old kid named Oshea Israel. Oshea served seventeen years in prison before being released. He now lives in his old neighborhood, remarkably right next door to Mary.

At first, Mary wanted justice. "He was an animal," she said. "He deserved to be caged."

Then, a few years ago Mary asked if she could meet her son's killer. She felt compelled to see if there was some way she could forgive him. After the first meeting took place, they met on a regular basis. When he got out of prison, she got an apartment for Oshea in her building. Not only in her building, but right next door.

Oshea, who now has a steady day job and is going to college at night, is still trying to forgive himself. And Mary, who has forgiven her son's killer, eloquently says, "Unforgiveness is like cancer. It will eat you from the inside out. It's not about that other person. Me forgiving him does not diminish what he's done. Yes, he murdered my son—but the forgiveness is for me. It's for me."

"Sometimes extending forgiveness can be incredibly hard," says Ira Byock, M.D., in his book *The Four Things that Matter Most.* "But," he continues, "forgiveness is always possible—and necessary—if people want to break free of the past and become healthy and whole."

As Mary discovered above, forgiveness is not about the other person; it's about you. "Whether or not the person who abused you benefits from your forgiveness, is not the issue," says Byock. "The issue is the quality of *your* life. Forgiveness is an act of affirmation on your part. It is a way of letting go of old wounds that weigh you down."

~~~~~~~~~~~~~~~~~~~~~~~~~~~~~~

The Keys to Happiness

"Are you hurt and suffering? Is the injury new, or is it an old unhealed wound? Know that what was done to you was wrong, unfair, and undeserved. You are right to be outraged. And it is perfectly normal to want to hurt back when you have been hurt. But hurting back rarely satisfies. We think it will, but it doesn't. If I slap you after you slap me, it does not lessen the sting I feel on my own face, nor does it diminish my sadness as to the fact you have struck me. Retaliation gives, at best, only momentary respite from our pain. The only way to experience healing and peace is to forgive. Until we can forgive, we remain locked in our pain and locked out of the possibility of experiencing healing and freedom, locked out of the possibility of being at peace.

"Without forgiveness, we remain tethered to the person who harmed us. We are bound with chains of bitterness, tied together, trapped. Until we can forgive the person who harmed us, that person will hold the keys to our happiness; that person will be our jailor. When we forgive, we take back control of our own fate and our feelings. We become our own liberators. We don't forgive to help the other person. We don't forgive for others. We forgive for ourselves."

—Desmond Tutu and Mpho Tutu,
The Book of Forgiving

Follow-Up

To err is human; to forgive, divine.

—ALEXANDER POPE,
English poet

I've read about one classroom teacher who visually demonstrates to her students how not forgiving someone can drag them down. She gives each student a sack of potatoes and asks them to write on each potato the names of someone they haven't forgiven—someone who perhaps has made them mad or angry, maybe bullied them or called them names. Then she asks them to put the potatoes in the sack and carry it around the room. Pretty soon the burden of carrying around the weight of not forgiving becomes clear.

If you have some potatoes in the house, you might want to try this powerful exercise. If you don't, try to imagine it and feel what it might be like to carry such a heavy load in your life day after day after day. And imagine how freeing it might be to get rid of the weight with a little bit of forgiveness.

Can I paraphrase a familiar saying here? "When life hands you a hot potato, make a potato pardon salad."

Lighten-Up

Once in a while, asking for forgiveness turns into a laughing matter. For example, here is an apology for an apology from a Canadian newspaper:

"The *Ottawa Citizen* and *Southam News* wish to apologize for our apology to Mark Steyn, published Oct. 22. In correcting the incorrect statements about Mr. Steyn published Oct. 15, we incorrectly published the incorrect correction. We accept and regret that our original regrets were unacceptable and we apologize to Mr. Steyn for any distress caused by our previous apology."

FORGIVE YOURSELF

⌘

Being gentle means forgiving yourself when you mess up. We should learn from our mistakes, but we shouldn't beat the tar out of ourselves over them. The past is just that, past. Learn what went wrong and why. Make amends if you need to. Then drop it and move on.

—SEAN COVEY,
football player

FORGIVENESS IS SUCH a major element in not letting anyone ruin your day that I have devoted two Wake-Up Calls to it. One focuses on forgiving others, and the other, perhaps even more important, is about forgiving yourself.

As hard as it is to forgive someone else, often it is easier to forgive him or her than to forgive yourself. Yet, if you want to have a great day, every day it is imperative to not only forgive others for an injustice they may have done to you but to also forgive yourself as well. "No one," says one clinical trainer in a drug and alcohol treatment center "can beat us up better than we beat ourselves up," as the following poignant story illustrates:

Thirty-seven years ago, a sixteen-year-old boy started meeting with his school friends for nights of drinking and drug taking. The raucous get-togethers took place for many years on a fairly regular basis. After one of these evenings, the teenager drove through a red light and straight into another car. He healed from his injuries in about three months, but for the man in the car he hit, it was much, much longer. In fact, the man is still not totally healed.

"There hasn't been a day in all those years," said the boy (now a man) who caused the accident, "that I haven't thought about what I did to another human being." With the help of a forgiveness program, he began to slowly come to terms with the pain and suffering he caused someone else. The program tracked down the man he injured, and they were able to meet face-to-face. After struggling with the idea for a long time, the former teenager finally apologized for the harm he had done.

In tears, he told the man how sorry he was. The injured man told him, "I forgave you a long time ago. Maybe it is time for you to finally forgive yourself."

A Forgiveness Exercise

While looking for an exercise about forgiving yourself, I found several funny tongue-in-cheek ones on a blog by Karen Rivers. Here is one I particularly liked:

"Go to a mirror. Stand in front of it. Do not be distracted by the color and texture of the skin on your winter-red cheeks. Talk to yourself as though you are someone you don't know. Try not to feel crazy. Do not moisturize. Not right now.

"Say the following words out loud: 'I forgive you' to yourself. Do not laugh. Do not under any circumstances begin fixing your hair, out of habit.

"Repeat the phrase, 'I forgive you' until it begins to sound like gibberish and you become worried the neighbors can hear you from the walkway and are preparing to call some sort of authorities to report the obvious loss of your mind.

"Sigh.

"Go ahead and wash your face. This isn't going to work."

Follow-Up

*One of the greatest struggles of the healing process
is to forgive both yourself and others and to stop
expending valuable energy on the past hurts.*

—CAROLINE MYSS,
author

When you first join a gym and lift weights, you don't pick up the heaviest ones first. You start with the lighter weights until you build your muscles up to handle the heavier ones. Forgiveness is similar to weight lifting. Whether forgiving yourself or someone else, start building your forgiveness muscle with smaller resentments and build up to handling the bigger ones.

You can start with these three steps for forgiving yourself:

- Pick something in your life that has upset you. It could involve a failed relationship, a family confrontation, or a business mistake, etc.

- In your mind, vividly relive the situation and make a list of anyone you might have hurt in that encounter. Be honest and take your time.

- Now forgive yourself or anyone you have hurt. Then,

as odd as it may sound, apologize out loud: "I forgive myself for hurting _____ (fill in the name of that person). Repeat the process with everyone on your list. Now take a deep breath and note how you feel.

Lighten-Up

The American comedian Emo Philips says this about forgiving himself: "When I was a kid I used to pray every night for a new bicycle. Then I realized that the Lord doesn't work that way so I stole one and asked Him to forgive me."

FIND THE GOOD NEWS IN THE BAD NEWS

⌘

Now that my house has burned down,
I can see the moon better.

—MASAHIDE,
Zen poet

WHEN I WAS a youngster, I remember being fascinated with a game that appeared in a magazine that came in the mail each month. It depicted such scenes as a park on a busy Sunday, a child playing in their room, or an intersection on Main Street. It looked pretty ordinary until you looked closer. Then you would notice, for example, that a bench in the park had only three legs, one of the toys in the bedroom was on the ceiling, or that someone was crossing the snowy street barefooted. The game was to find as many of these out-of-place things as possible. It kept me busy for hours.

Finding some good news in a not-so-great situation is like that game. Sometimes you may have to look a little closer or a little longer, and sometimes you may have to look real hard, but it is usually there. For example, the death of someone could be a time of sadness, but it could also be a blessing if they were ill and in pain for a long time and are no longer suffering. Or, someone who has been fired from their job might be angry, but it might also be a time to seek employment that brings them greater fulfillment and a boss who doesn't yell and put them down all the time.

Looking for the good in the bad is not to deny your pain or your upset; it is about not letting your setbacks prevent you from recognizing the positive potential in the situation.

My mother, for example, found some good news in the bad news when she was moving to a new apartment. While packing, she had taken too many dishes out of a cabinet and put them on a flimsy folding table. It collapsed, breaking half the dishes. When she told me about the incident, and I started to sympathize with her loss, she quickly stopped me. And, on a positive note, she said, "Well, now I have less to pack."

Thomas Edison too saw some good in the not-so-good news when a fire destroyed his manufacturing facility. He lost almost one million dollars in equipment and much of the writings about his inventions. After reviewing the wreckage, he noted, "There is value in disaster. All our mistakes are burned up. Now we can start anew."

Starting anew is a wonderful thing to remember when your day is not going well. Each month, each week, each day, each hour, each minute is an opportunity for a fresh start. Perhaps it is why so many people make New Year's resolutions. They realize that the beginning of the year is a great time to put the past year behind them and start anew.

But you don't have to wait for a new year. Right now you can transform your upsets and see them in a new way by looking for the good in the not-so-good.

And, one more thing, actually a piece of good news: Recent research has documented that finding something good in a situation is good for your health. At the University of Connecticut, psychologist Glenn Affleck interviewed 287 people who were recovering from a heart attack. He discovered that those who found a benefit in being ill were less likely to suffer a second heart attack.

~~~~~~~~~~~~~~~~~~~~~~~~~~

Life as a Joyful Adventure

"Our life has become a collection of solutions to a problem we do not have.

"Let us look at it another way. Being born is like waking up inside a dream and not knowing it. In our sleep we have amassed a garrison of devices and decisions to protect ourselves from the threat from outside.... We have barricaded ourselves in our cabin to fight off the [attackers] while we wait in fervent hope for the cavalry to arrive and save us.

"Well, I have good news and I have bad news. First, the bad news: the cavalry isn't coming. Sorry, but Rin Tin Tin, John Wayne, and the detachment from Fort Apache are not going to come riding over the hill. No one is going to save us from the [attackers] of our life.

"When we really get the hopelessness of that fact, it may make us very sad. It will also allow us to get the good news. And the good news is, there aren't any [attackers]. There is only a universe that supports us in making life a joyful adventure or an endless nightmare. So while there is no hope, it is also true that there is no hope needed."

—Stewart Emery,
author of *Actualizations*

Follow-Up

The good news is that Jesus is coming back. The bad news is that he's really pissed off.

—BOB HOPE,
comedian

This week, see if you can do the reverse of a good news/ bad news scenario. Instead of starting with good news and concluding with bad news, as usually happens in this type of joke, start with the bad news and see if you can find some good news in it. For example:

- The bad news is I have to pay a lot of taxes this year. The good news is that I must have made a lot of money last year.

- The bad news is I'm losing my hair. The good news is I can save time brushing it and save money not having to buy shampoos and conditioners.

- The bad news is that I've been stuck in traffic for three hours. The good news is I didn't really want to go to that meeting anyway.

Lighten-Up

Doctor: I have some good news and I have some bad news.

Patient: What's the good news?

Doctor: The good news is that the tests you took showed that you have twenty-four hours to live.

Patient: That's the good news? What's the bad news?

Doctor: The bad news is that I forgot to call you yesterday!

PUT IT IN NEUTRAL

⌘

Many think that the law of non-resistance is being weak or a doormat. Nothing could be further from the truth. Non-resistance is not indifference; it is not a sign of weakness or ignorance. Non-resistance is stronger than resistance, it is powerful, and to actively engage in non-resistance takes great aware-ness, love, practice, and bravery.

—NANCY NORMAN,
Unity minister

MANY PEOPLE THINK that the world is out to get them. If you are one of those people, stop that thinking right now! The world is not out to get you. Situations are what they are. You are the one who sees something as suffocating or supporting you. When you feel that you are a target, you will naturally feel victimized. But there is another way to look at what is happening to you, no matter what that is. It is to see everything from a neutral point of view.

If you put your car in neutral gear, it detaches the transmission from the motor. Putting a difficult situation in neutral is like that; it will detach you from your upset.

Many people today also say that they are "stressed out" without realizing that they are the ones creating the stress. Stress is an inside job. Flying on a plane, for example, might be a great joy for one person, stressful for another. The anticipation of preparing to take a vacation, or even getting married, might be a joyous occasion for one person but stressful for another.

In his book, *You Can Be Happy No Matter What*, author Richard Carlson provides another illustration using the example of a circus coming to town. He writes, "For people and families who love the circus, this is a great cause for celebration. For those who don't love the circus, the increased traffic and confusion causes concern. The circus itself is neutral—it isn't the cause of positive or negative reactions."

All of these examples, as well as other situations in life are neutral. They are not, in and of themselves, stressful. We are the ones who label them as such. It is our perception of the situation that makes them so. As Carlson reminds us, "Circumstances are always neutral. If they were the cause of our problems, they would always affect us in the same way, which of course they don't."

Years ago I had the opportunity to practice staying neutral. My schedule got so busy that I neglected to keep in touch with one of my best friends. For three months, I did not call or write him. As a result, he sat me down one day and read me a long list of why he never wanted to see me again. As I recall, he had over seventy items on the list.

I was stunned by his breakup of our long friendship, but I also realized that nearly everything he was telling me was true: I didn't return his calls; I didn't send him a birthday card; I didn't come to his garage sale, etc.

My friend was extremely angry and wanted me to defend myself and fight back, but I did the opposite. I agreed with most of what he said. Moreover, instead of being confrontational, I told him that anyone who had given so much time and thought to our relationship must really love me. Instead of adding fuel to a volatile situation, I stayed neutral. I didn't get angry or become defensive.

As radio commentator Paul Harvey used to say, "And now for the rest of the story."

My friend and I are good friends once again and frequently joke about the "I-Never-Want-to-See-You-Again" list. Now when either of us does something that irritates the other, we call out what the next number might be on the list and have a good laugh.

Staying neutral is a great way to not get caught up in daily upsets, irritations, and aggravations. It can also help us see more clearly. In my own life, for example, I saw how staying neutral actually led me to my current career as a professional speaker and author.

When my wife died, I was co-owner of a silkscreen company. After her death, I realized that silk-screening was not what I was supposed to be doing in my life, but I had no idea what the right thing was. So I just hung out. I sold my share of the silk-screen business to my partner and waited for the universe to direct me.

Then, one day, a brochure came from Holistic Life University. They had a life-death transition division. Since no one that close to me had ever died before, I enrolled in the course to learn about death and dying. After a couple of years, I became the head of the program as well as a hospice volunteer and a licensed home health aide. Over and over again I saw how patients would use humor to cope. So I went back to college to learn about therapeutic humor, got a master's degree in the subject, and started to write and speak about it.

I can credit my twenty-plus years in the therapeutic humor field to a combination of stopping what I was doing, which wasn't fulfilling my soul, and waiting, becoming neutral, if you will, for my inner being to direct me to what I was supposed to be doing.

I believe that there is some power within us, call it what you will—God, Jesus, Spirit, etc.—that is there to guide us toward the highest good. But when we battle life and the situations we face, instead of flowing with them, we are going against our true nature and the forces of the universe.

Seeing things from a neutral place is a major shift from

playing the victim to taking back your personal power and not letting anyone or anything ruin your day.

Try it and see what happens.

Follow-Up

Handle every stressful situation like a dog. If you can't eat it or play with it, pee on it and walk away.

—ANONYMOUS

Here are three "put-it-in-neutral" things you can do right now to prevent others from ruining your day:

1. *Give up being right.* Insisting that you are right, even if you are, makes the other person wrong. In the book *A Course in Miracles,* there is a profound, yet simple, question: "Do you want to be right or do you want to be happy?" Which one you choose, right or happy, will set the tone for what kind of day you will have.

2. *Use a green lens.* Clinical psychologist Maria Nemeth suggests that we view other people through a "green lens" rather than a red one, which views people in a negative way. Nemeth's green lens view of people, on the other hand, presents a way of seeing others in a more positive way. For example:

This person is a hero, whole and complete.

This person has goals and dreams and a desire to make a difference.

This person has his/her own answers.

This person is contributing to me right now.

This person deserves to be treated with dignity and respect.

3. *Ask one simple question.* There are three words that can help you not get caught up in an argument or other people's stuff. When you find yourself about to entangle with someone who is angry and yelling at you, stop and ask them: "Tell me more." Repeat as needed.

Lighten-Up

Sometimes I get the feeling the whole world is against me, but deep down I know that's not true. Some of the smaller countries are neutral.

—ROBERT ORBEN,
comedy writer

I love Zen teaching stories because they not only vividly make their point ("ah-ha") but also often have a lightness about them ("ha-ha") that make them easier to digest. One such story revolves around putting things in neutral and

Allen Klein

not getting caught up in the "mishugas" (a Yiddish word meaning "crazy" or "craziness") of the world.

An old farmer worked his crops for many years. One day his horse ran away. Upon hearing the news, his neighbors came to visit.

"Such bad luck," they said sympathetically.

"We'll see," the farmer replied.

The next morning the horse returned, bringing with it three other wild horses.

"How wonderful," the neighbors exclaimed.

"We'll see," replied the old farmer.

The following day, his son tried to ride one of the untamed horses, was thrown and broke his leg. The neighbors again came to offer their sympathy on his misfortune. "We'll see," answered the farmer.

The day after, military officials came to the village to draft young men into the army. Seeing that the son's leg was broken, they passed him by. The neighbors congratulated the farmer on how well things had turned out.

"We'll see," said the farmer.

PUT IT IN PERSPECTIVE

⌘

*I wish the whole world could see what I see. Some-
times you have to go up really high to understand how
small we really are.*

—FELIX BAUMGARTNER,
skydiver

A COLLEAGUE OF mine recently found out that she had
cancer. To keep her friends and family informed of how she
was doing, as well as her progress with chemo treatments,
she posted regular updates on an Internet site specifically
set up for that purpose.

On one post, she noted, "I just wrote a wonderful new
update for you and then the site crashed and I lost it. So,
here we go again. Doubtful I'll remember what I said, but I'll

try. The interesting thing is—it's not a big deal. It's like once you get something like cancer, small stuff doesn't seem so important."

Another colleague of mine, Randy Gage, also talked about what is important in our life and what is not. He posted these perspective-provoking questions on his blog:

"Is the fact someone was careless and inadvertently cut you off on the highway worth blowing the horn, swearing, and raising your blood pressure?"

"Is getting overcharged two dollars at the supermarket worth a trip back? Or would you be better spending the time earning another fifty?"

"If your spouse is loving, loyal, and caring—is it really a hill to die on that they squeeze the toothpaste in the middle of the tube?"

Changing your perspective need not be a big move. Earlier in the book, I spoke about Timothy Wilson's research showing how just a small change in the story you tell yourself, or the world, can make a big difference in how you see a stressful situation.

Just the other day I was presented with a great example of how a minor change made a major difference. I was in the kitchen and just used a potholder to take a hot dish out of the microwave oven. I put the dish down on the counter to do something else for a moment then returned to move the dish to the table. But I could not find the potholder. I stood there for several minutes, scanned the kitchen, but did not see it.

How could the potholder disappear when I just put it down? Then I moved one step to the left and saw it peeking out from a partially overturned pot lid.

From one angle it was impossible to see the potholder. Changing my perspective and moving just slightly to one side allowed me to see the situation in a different way.

Life is like that too. We see it from only one angle, one perspective. Change that angle, sometimes even just slightly, and things can appear totally differently.

Next time someone pisses you off, mentally take a half step sideways and see him or her from a different angle. See their good side. See that they have wants and needs just like you. See that they are not out to get you; they are just people with a different opinion than yours. See them as an ally instead of an enemy.

~~~~~~~~~~~~~~~~~~~~~~~~~~~~~~~

Looking Through a Lens

Dave Cooperberg, the San Francisco therapist I mentioned earlier, does a process with his patients in which he has them look out the window on a sunny day. First he has them view the scene through a pair of dark wraparound sunglasses. Next, he asks them to put on a bright pink pair and asks, "Which view do you prefer?"

Generally, his clients report that things look dull and dreary with the dark gray pair. Most clients prefer looking through the bright pink glasses, even though neither pair is a true representation of the scene out the window. The process, however, illustrates how much one's attitude affects our view of life. "Our perspective," says Cooperberg, "influences what we see. The more one can learn and choose to see the bright side, the more one's life will feel lighter and more enjoyable."

Bruce H. Lipton describes a similar process in his book, *The Biology of Belief*, in which he has the audience view a scene using either a red or green lens. He then asks the audience to call out either "I live in love" or "I live in fear." Depending on which lens they are looking through, some people see love, others fear.

"My point is," says Lipton, "that you can choose what to see.... You can live a life of fear or live a life of love.... But I can tell you that if you choose to see a world full of love, your body will respond by growing in health. If you choose to believe that you live in a dark world full of fear, your body's health will be compromised as you physiologically close yourself down in a protection response."

~~~~~~~~~~~~~~~~~~~~~~~~~~~~

Follow-Up

Reversing how you look at a situation can dislodge assumptions and open up new possibilities. Example: Spend a minute describing a problem you're working on. If you are a male, describe it from the viewpoint of a female. If you're a female, describe it from a male viewpoint.

—ROGER VON OECH,
Creative Whack Pack

In the evening, review the day you just experienced. Write down the most annoying, irritating, or upsetting thing that happened to you. Now see it from a different perspective: How might a child see your trying situation? Your favorite comedian? Your grandmother? Your favorite movie star? Your first grade schoolteacher?

Lighten-Up

Dear Mom and Dad,

I am sorry that I have not written, but all my stationery was destroyed when the dorm burned down. I am now out of the hospital and the doctor said that I will recover soon. I have also moved in with the boy who rescued me, since most of my things were destroyed in the fire.

Oh yes, I know that you have always wanted a grandchild, so you will be pleased to know that I am pregnant and you will have one soon.

Love,
Mary

Then there was a postscript:

P.S. There was no fire, my health is perfectly fine, and I am not pregnant. In fact, I don't even have a boyfriend. But I did get a D in French and a C in math and chemistry, and I just wanted to make sure that you keep it all in perspective.

TAKE THE FIVE-MINUTE, FIVE-MONTH, FIVE-YEAR TEST

⌘

*We can only be said to be alive in those moments
when our hearts are conscious of our treasures.*

—THORNTON WILDER,
playwright

IN HIS PULITZER Prize–winning play, *Our Town*, Thornton
Wilder writes about a young woman named Emily who dies
and goes to heaven. On her first day there, she wants to
return to earth in order to experience it just one more time.
She is given the choice of selecting any day in her life. She
chooses the day when she turned twelve.

Emily watches as her mother makes breakfast and notices
all the things she took for granted when she was alive...the
sunflowers...the food...the coffee...the newly ironed dresses...

the hot baths...and sleeping and waking up. "Do any human beings," Emily poignantly asks, "ever realize life while they live it?"

There is so much distraction around us that life often passes us by without us noticing the small fleeting moments that are what life is really all about. This was movingly portrayed in a production I saw a few years ago of *Our Town*. The smell of bacon that Emily's mother was actually cooking on stage filled the theater and reminded us of a similar delicious, and perhaps ignored, moment in our own lives.

A delightful friend and colleague of mine, who lives in Hawaii, Pat Masumoto, shares "A Simple Pleasure" on a regular basis on her Facebook page. What I like about that, and something that she may not even realize herself, is that committing to post almost every day forces her to find something pleasurable in her life on a daily basis. And, by doing so, she has also inspired us to do the same thing. Some of Masumoto's simple pleasures include: spraying lavender water on her face; watching the moon become the color of translucent copper; enjoying homemade coconut-chocolate ice cream; making chicken soup Asian style, with bamboo shoots, water chestnuts, shiitake mushrooms... and sprinkled with fresh grated ginger, green onions, and chili peppers; and sleeping on a bed in the room where she was born.

And even after both her mother and her son died within less than a month of each other, she still continued to post

"A Simple Pleasure": Feeling loved by those who share in my grief, feeling grateful to laugh with them about the "foibles" of life.

This week, the challenges and struggles you are facing are probably distracting you from noticing the small but pleasurable moments in your life. Those delicious instances are always there but when you are stressed out, you don't see them.

So this week, try seeing your difficulties in a new way. Instead of getting upset over them, see them as wake-up calls reminding you to pay attention to those precious pleasurable moments. This week, see if you can stop and smell the bacon!

~~~~~~~~~~~~~~~~~~~~~~~~~~~~~

Think Like a Hawaiian

Speaking about simple pleasures reminds me of a story my friend and professional speaking colleague Steve Rizzo told me about the lesson he learned while in Hawaii:

"One morning, two hours before my speech, I was having breakfast at a restaurant with a captivating view of the ocean. As the waitress was pouring my coffee, I asked, 'Why is it no matter where they are, or what they are doing, Hawaiian people always seem to be happy and at peace with themselves? Is there some kind of secret that I should know about? And if there is, can you please tell me?'

"She laughed and looked around as if to make sure that no one was listening and in a low voice she replied, 'Mr. Rizzo, today is your lucky day. For today I will tell you the secret that most Hawaiian people live by.' She sat down in the chair next to me, motioned me to get closer, and whispered in my ear, 'We learn to dance in the rain.'

"Before I had a chance to respond, she reached into her pocket and pulled out a laminated card and handed it to me and said, 'This is for you. It really is a secret that should be shared with everyone—Don't wait for the storms of your life to pass. Learn to dance in the rain.'"

Follow-Up

Sometimes things in life happen that allow us to understand our priorities very clearly. Ultimately you can see those as gifts.

—MARISKA HARGITAY,
actress

In taxing times, when it feels like someone or something is ruining your day, you might want to ask yourself, "How will this situation, which I am letting ruin my day, look like in five minutes, five months, or five years from now?" When you look back from that perspective, might that supposedly troublesome situation be seen differently?

Lighten-Up

A man walked into a gift shop that sold religious items. Near the cash register he saw a display of caps with "WWJD" printed on all of them. He was puzzled over what the letters could mean, but couldn't figure it out, so he asked the clerk.

The clerk replied that the letters stood for "What Would Jesus Do?" It was meant to inspire people to not make rash decisions, but rather to imagine what Jesus would do in the same situation.

The man thought a moment and then replied, "Well, I'm damn sure Jesus wouldn't pay $19.95 for one of these caps."

PART TWO

WISE-UP

If you're trying to achieve, there will be roadblocks. I've had them; everybody has had them. But obstacles don't have to stop you. If you run into a wall, don't turn around and give up. Figure out how to climb it, go through it, or work around it.

—MICHAEL JORDAN,
basketball player

SAY "YES"

⌘

If the shutters are closed, the sunlight cannot come in.

—ECKHART TOLLE,
author and spiritual teacher

YEARS AGO, I took an improvisation class. Improvisation is the art of creating something from whatever is presented to you. One of the things we learned, which is a cornerstone of improvisational technique, was called "Yes, and…" It means that one of the improvisers will say or do something and, without rejecting it, the other improviser will accept it and add something new to the action. Basically, it is a method of being willing to accept and say "yes" to what is given to you.

Before you can have anything change in your life, you have to be willing for it to change. I'm going to repeat that because it is an extremely simple concept but a difficult one to fully comprehend: "Before you can have anything change in your life, you have to be willing for it to change." The key words here are *be willing*.

Things don't change by themselves; there has to be some energy to get things moving. If you want something to be other than the way it is, the first question you need to ask yourself is "Am I willing?"

"Am I willing for things to change?

"Am I willing for things to be other than what I perceive them to be now?"

"Am I willing not to let anything or anyone upset me?"

"Am I willing to put annoyances aside today?"

"Am I willing to not insist on being right all the time?"

"Am I willing to change my view of a hostile world into a world that supports me in everything I do?"

"Am I willing to not let others ruin my day?"

Saying *yes* to these things may not be comfortable; in fact it may be very difficult. But if you want to move from where you are now, to a better place where you take back your power and control your day and your life, then you must be willing to say *yes* in spite of the discomfort.

When I wanted to be a professional speaker, sharing my message about the therapeutic value of humor was not easy. I almost failed speech class in college so getting up in front of a group was terrifying. But saying *yes* and being willing to do whatever it took empowered me to rise above my fear and share my message anyway. Saying *yes* also empowered me to get my first book published when others told me it was impossible.

Being willing and saying *yes* can empower you too to face your current roadblocks.

~~~~~~~~~~~~~~~~~~~~~~~~~

The Only Direction Is Forward

"'Is this bigger than me, or am I bigger than it?' In other words, 'Do I have what it takes? Do I have the resources, skill, experience, or the energy to take on this change and succeed?' If we answer 'no,' we are more likely to back away from the challenge and focus on what could go wrong, or what we could lose.

"If, however, we answer 'yes,' we'll go after the challenge as if there's no tomorrow. Our hopeful perspective creates a compelling mental image of what success looks like. We'll tap into our strengths and know-how with determination, while continuing to 'grow bigger' with each forward step. 'I can do this! I might not know how at this moment, but I'll figure it out.'

"I've had the privilege of witnessing an inspiring example of what a 'yes' answer looks like over the last month. A friend's husband unexpectedly passed away, leaving her to raise their two young children on her own. Along with this uninvited change, she is now the sole breadwinner, decision-maker, and problem-solver. In a conversation with her a few days ago I asked her how she was doing, and she replied, 'While I've shed my share of tears, I am choosing to not put myself in a corner and cry. Life has to go on, and the only direction for me is forward.'"

—Lauri Gwilt,
Celebrate What's Right with the World blog

Follow-Up

If you tell God no because He won't explain the reason He wants you to do something, you are actually hindering His blessing. But when you say yes to Him, all of heaven opens to pour out His goodness and reward your obedience.

—CHARLES STANLEY,
religious leader

This week see if you can say *yes* to things in situations where you have previously said *no*. Then notice if anything has changed...if your day is richer...if you are less defensive than you have been.

Lighten-Up

*I went down the street to the 24-hour grocery. When
I got there, the guy was locking the front door. I said,
"Hey, the sign says you're open 24 hours." He said,
"Yes, but not in a row."*

—STEVEN WRIGHT,
comedian

An eager and willing, but less than bright, young entrepreneur decides to go into the painting business. So he goes to a wealthy part of town, paintbrush in hand, and knocks at the door of a large house.

"Good day, sir. I was wondering if you had any painting you need to have done."

The owner of the house, a rich man by any standard, looks speculatively at the painter. He perceives a vibrant entrepreneurial spirit, which reminds him of his own ambition in his younger days.

"Hmmm. Yes, I think my porch needs a coat or two of paint."

The eager young painter rushes off around the side of the house.

Several hours later, he returns to the front door, his clothes dripping paint, and knocks again.

"Sir, I've finished! But I have to tell you, that wasn't a porch, it was a Ferrari."

SET YOUR INTENTION

⌘

At the moment of commitment, the entire universe
conspires to assist you.

—GOETHE,
German writer and statesman

WHEN I WAS a teenager, I never heard about the power of the mind to create what we want to have happen or the power of intention. Yet that is exactly what I did one day.

A distant relative of mine was being bar mitzvahed. I don't recall why but I did not want to go to the synagogue or the party afterward. I suspect it was because I either didn't really like him or I was too shy at the time and knew I'd have to interact with a lot of people that day.

Several times during the week, I told my parents that

I didn't want to go to the event on Saturday. Mostly they ignored me but on Saturday morning, when I woke up with a 102-degree fever, they said that, of course, I could not go. So, I stayed in bed all day. When my parents came home, my mom took my temperature to see how I was doing. I no longer had a fever. I was perfectly fine.

I'm not sure what I did, or how I did it. All I know, looking back, is that it was my intention not to go to the bar mitzvah and I somehow created a fever that prevented me from doing so. The power of intention!

On her blog, health coach Aimee DuFresne has a wonderful story about intention and what she calls, "making a space for the impossible." She writes:

"When I grow up, I am going to marry an American woman. And she is going to propose to me."

Sitting under a tree with his sister and two brothers and in front of his home in the south of France, a little boy said these words with utter certainty.

At that same time in America, a little girl sat quietly with her brother in his bedroom as they watched a show on the television in French. Neither of them understanding the language, but wanting to learn it. The little girl dreamed of going to France one day. It seemed like the most magical place.

Fast-forward a few decades...give or take.

There is the tree.

And there is the American girl who proposed to the boy

and traveled with him to France (a most magical place) to celebrate their life and marriage.

True story.

Funny how life works out, isn't it?

Sometimes you set an intention without realizing it—or without realizing how powerful it is. At the time it might seem far-fetched, improbable, or even impossible if you try to figure out all the logistics of the "how" and "when" of it all.

But when you are a kid, the "how" and "when" seem insignificant.

You are much more likely to just go with what you know to be true. Even if it isn't true just yet.

And perhaps that makes the intentions you set then even more powerful.

What if you were to be as free as a kid again, dreaming big with certainty and without the fear and doubt that comes along with figuring out the "how" and "when" of it all?

What if the far-fetched was within your reach?

What if the improbable would probably happen?

What if, instead of thinking it's impossible, you thought: I'm possible (after all, it's the same letters, it just requires a little space).

The bottom line is that by setting your intention for what you want, including not letting anyone or anything ruin your day, you set the tone for it to possibly happen. The New Thought spiritual teachings of Abraham, as channeled through Esther Hicks, says that "by setting your Tone in a clear deliberate way, anything that doesn't match it gravitates out of your experience, and anything that does match it gravitates into your experience. It is so much simpler," continues the teaching, "than most of you are allowing yourself to believe."

~~~~~~~~~~~~~~~~~~~~~~~~~~

Take the First Step

There is a story about an elephant in a circus who was chained to a stump its entire life. When the circus burned down, someone cut the elephant's chains so that it could escape. The elephant, having known nothing else but being chained to a stump, remained where it was and died in the fire.

I don't know if this story is true or not, nevertheless, it speaks to an important issue. Nothing happens unless you take the first step. You can get all the advice from all the gurus in the world but if you do what you have always done, you will always get what you always got. Like the stuck elephant, it is up to you, and only you, to take the first step.

What have you been putting off or meaning to do for perhaps a long time? This week would be an excellent time to begin whatever that is. And if you still feel resistance, try setting an alarm or kitchen timer for, say, fifteen minutes and begin your task. Then stop when the bell rings. At least you will know, and perhaps feel some sense of satisfaction, that you have taken the first step.

~~~~~~~~~~~~~~~~~~~~~~~~~~~~~~

Follow-Up

If your intention is to be loving and caring, you cannot let anything that is not loving or caring come into your field of action.

—JOHN-ROGER,
spiritual teacher

In the long-running musical, *The Fantasticks*, there is a song about planting a radish in order to get a radish, not some other vegetable. It is a great metaphor and reminder for us to plant only the seeds of what we want to harvest. Your intentions are the seeds that you are sowing. What are you planting?

In his book, *The Code: 10 Intentions for a Better World*, author Tony Burroughs provides some suggestions for what he calls the "intention process." Here are a few that you might want to consider: There is power in the spoken word. Saying our intentions out loud focuses our thoughts. Positive thoughts bring positive experiences. Negative thoughts bring undesired experiences. Ask that in order for our intentions to come to us, they must serve the highest and best good for the Universe and the highest and best good for ourselves and for others.

What is your intention today? Write it down and keep it positive. Avoid writing down something you don't want to happen. For example, instead of writing, "Today I will *not* be stressed out," put down, "Today I will be stress-free." Eliminate such words as trying, hoping, wanting, etc. Only write down what you want to happen. For example, "Today I will have fun." "Today I will be happy."

My Intention for Today:

1. Make sure nobody ruins my day.

2. See #1.

In order to do that you might want to strengthen your intention by taking the following pledge:

Raise your right hand and put your left index finger on your nose. Then say out loud: "Starting right now, I will take back my power and not let anyone, or any situation, ruin my day. So help me, Oprah Winfrey."

Lighten-Up

A young man wanted to purchase a gift for his new sweetie for Valentine's Day. As they had not been dating very long, it was a difficult decision. After careful consideration he decided a good gift would be a pair of gloves.

Accompanied by his sister, he went to the store and bought the gloves. His sister purchased a pair of panties at the same time. The clerk carefully wrapped both items but in the process got them mixed up. The sister was handed the gloves and the young man got the panties.

The young man mailed his Valentine's Day gift with the following note:

"This special Valentine's Day gift was chosen because I noticed you are in the habit of not wearing any when we go out in the evenings. If it had not been for my sister, I would have chosen the ones with buttons, but she prefers short ones that are much easier to remove. The lady I bought them from showed me the pair she had been wearing for the past three weeks and they were hardly soiled. I had her try yours on for me, and they looked quite lovely. I wish I were there to put them on you for the first time. Just think how many times I'll be kissing them in the future. I hope you'll wear them Friday night for me."

STOP STRUGGLING

⌘

When you are relaxed and flexible, you are happy;
when you are rigid and controlling, you are unhappy.
So the key is letting go of the urge to get people to
behave and events to go your way.

—HUGH PRATHER,
author and minister

Do you remember a toy called a Chinese finger puzzle or Chinese finger trap? It was a small woven bamboo cylinder. When you put your index fingers in each end, it was difficult to get them out again. The harder you pulled, the more you got stuck. The only way to get them out was to stop struggling, stop resisting, relax and let go.

Anger, being upset, and frustration are like that. The

more you get trapped in them, the harder it is to escape. One of the tricks for ending those states of mind is, as with the Chinese finger trap, to stop struggling, relax, and let go.

One of today's biggest irritations, one that can ruin any day, is lack of control. Take traffic jams, for example. Drivers get stressed out big time when they are stuck in them because they can't control the situation. The same is true of airline passengers who get bent out of shape because they can't control weather-related delays or cancellations. Or office workers who stress out because they feel trapped in large bureaucracies or corporations with little or no control over their jobs. Still others get trapped in relationships that don't work.

Life provides endless examples of things we can't control. But, we can get an upper hand on them by not letting them outfox us. Mind you, I didn't say change them. We can't change traffic jams, the weather, or other people's decisions that affect us. But, like the Chinese finger trap, the more you resist, the more things persist. If you want to have a great day today, let go and stop resisting.

"Resistance," says Nancy Norman, the Unity minister quoted in Wake-Up Call #11, "keeps us in bondage, causes turmoil, strife, unhappiness, (as well as) mental, emotional, physical, and psychological pain…. We sometimes feel the need to fight back, to justify or explain, only to find that the difficulty continues to expand as we resist another's opinion about us. If we resist them or fight back, it only puts us on the same level we consider them to be."

To be happier and not let anyone ruin your day, the secret of life is to not take anything personally, to let go and to stop resisting.

~~~~~~~~~~~~~~~~~~~~~~~~~~~~~

Make a List

In her book, *The Observation Deck*, author Naomi Epel presents techniques writers have used to get their creative juices flowing when they were struggling with their writing. One of those is to make a list. Science fiction writer Ray Bradbury, for example, made lists of nouns; Thomas Wolfe filled ledgers with lists of names of places and things he'd observed.

"If you are trying to solve a...problem," Epel advises, "make a list of ten or twenty possibilities rather than straining to find the perfect solution. Some can be mundane, some silly, some downright stupid, but in releasing all those thoughts onto paper, you can free the two or three brilliant ones trapped behind the others."

You may not be a writer but making a list can help you deal with situations with which you are struggling. If you are angry with someone, make a list of things you can do to abate your anger without being hostile toward that person. If you are mad about a situation, make a list of things that might calm you down.

~~~~~~~~~~~~~~~~~~~~~~~~~~~~~

Follow-Up

So many things happen for every event, and if you try to manipulate it, it means you are struggling against the whole universe, and that's just silly.

—DEEPAK CHOPRA,
author

Years ago when I was designing the *Captain Kangaroo* show on CBS Television, I had to come up with some way of affixing numerous cardboard cutouts to the wall behind the puppet stage. The previous designer used magnets to hold them in place but they often scratched the surface resulting in the need for it to be repainted almost every day. To cut down on that expense, I searched for a product that would hold the cutout in place without damaging the wall.

I discovered a newly introduced product on the market called Velcro˚. It was perfect. The hook-and-loop fastening system allowed things to instantly grip and remain stuck until they were dislodged.

I tell you this story because, like Velcro˚, we often get stuck to things, irritations that instantly take hold of us and refuse to let go. We can, however, let them go more easily if we think of them in relationship to another fairly new invention—Teflon˚, the "non-stick" surface used in cookware.

Every day, when you encounter an irritating occurrence that is seemingly ruining your day, you can either let it stick to you like Velcro®, or, like Teflon®, let it simply glide right off you.

What do you need to stop resisting today in order to have a great day? With your family...your spouse...your kids? At work...with your coworker...your boss? In the world...with people or situations you encounter?

Can you take any of these annoyances and step back, stop resisting, and not get caught up in the situation? To help you do that today, when those circumstances arise, ask yourself, "Am I going to be a Velcro® or a Teflon® person?"

Lighten-Up

One foggy night, a United States aircraft carrier was cruising off the coast of Newfoundland and the junior radar operator spotted a light in the darkness.

The radar person worked out that a collision was likely unless the other vessel changed its course. So he sent a radio message. Below is a transcript of what happened next:

"Please divert your course at least seven degrees to the south to avoid a collision."

Back came the reply: "You must be joking, I recommend you divert your course instead."

The radar officer referred the matter to his superior

officer. And reported the incident as insubordination.

As a result the captain of the aircraft carrier sent a second message: "I believe that I outrank you, and am giving you a direct order to divert your course now!"

"This is a lighthouse. Your call."

LOOK OUT FOR THE LITTLE THINGS

⌘

Every day we have plenty of opportunities to get angry, stressed, or offended. But what you're doing when you indulge these negative emotions is giving something outside yourself power over your happiness. You can choose to not let little things upset you.

—JOEL OSTEEN,
preacher

WHEN I WAS first starting out on my speaking career, I heard a wonderful speaker whose message I still remember from some twenty years ago. His name was Joel Weldon and the title of his talk was "Elephants Don't Bite." I recall him asking the audience if a mosquito or some other small insect had ever bitten them. Nearly everyone in the audience raised their hand. Then he asked, "Anyone ever been bitten by an elephant?" Of course, this time no hands went up. Weldon then made his point, "It's the little things that get you, not the big ones."

Drew Gerber, CEO of a publicity company, knew exactly what Weldon was talking about when he found himself extremely annoyed on a flight where the attendants were not serving the coffee fast enough.

"Interestingly," notes Gerber, "the passengers around me didn't seem annoyed at all; they were simply enjoying the flight. Weird, I thought. Perhaps they'd all had coffee in the airport—the only possible explanation for their bizarre behavior."

"The more I caught on to what was happening (or *wasn't* happening), the slower the staff seemed to move. You know the saying, 'A watched pot never boils'?"

Gerber's point is that "most of us live like it's the 'big things' in life that throw us off our game...being fired, having an argument with our spouse, not being able to take the vacation we want, when we want, etc. But if we really look closely, those big things are actually the *easiest* things to deal with because we know that they're there. But have you noticed that it's the little thoughts—like not getting our coffee fast enough, like being assigned the middle seat, having to stand in line, or having to work late...you get the point—that grab our attention and begin to take us into the bad neighborhood unknowingly?"

"What I am saying," notes Gerber, "is that those little

things don't have to color our whole world. It *is* possible to wait for our coffee *and* enjoy the flight."

He concludes, "It wasn't even good coffee!"

Follow-Up

Don't let negative and toxic people rent space in your head. Raise the rent and kick them out!

—ROBERT TEW
(attributed)

Did some little thing bug you or tee you off today? Well, you are not alone. I just found a site on the Internet, getannoyed.com, which lists more than six hundred small things that get on most people's nerves. I won't list all of them here because it would take about eight pages. But just looking at this vast list made me chuckle. The reason I started to laugh is because some of them seem so trivial in the bigger picture of life.

A few that I randomly spotted were: whistling out of tune; lawn ornaments; dull pencils; backward toilet paper rolls; bread cut only halfway, at a restaurant, instead of into slices.

You might want to start an ongoing list of your own annoying things this week to see how small or humorous they seem when viewed several days after they occurred.

Lighten-Up

When southern Florida resident Nathan Radlich's house was burglarized, thieves ignored his wide-screen plasma TV, his VCR, and even his Rolex watch. What they did take, however, was a white box filled with a grayish-white powder. (That's the way the police report described it.)

A spokesman for the Fort Lauderdale police said that it looked similar to high-grade cocaine and the burglars probably thought they'd hit the big time.

Later, Nathan stood in front of numerous TV cameras and pleaded with the burglars: "Please return the cremated remains of my sister, Gertrude. She died three years ago." The next morning, the bullet-riddled corpse of a local drug dealer known as Hoochie Pevens was found on Nathan's doorstep. The white box was there too; about half of Gertrude's ashes remained.

Scotch-taped to the box was this note: "Hoochie sold us the bogus blow, so we wasted Hoochie. Sorry we snorted your sister. No hard feelings. Have a nice day."

GIVE UP PERFECTION

⌘

I spent a lot of years striving to be perfect. I even went so far as to clean under my toilet bowl since my mother convinced me that someone might check it out. I realized one day that no one that short was ever coming over.

—LORETTA LAROCHE,
author and speaker

ONE OF THE things that can quickly ruin your day is insisting that everything be perfect. Sorry folks, but it will probably never happen. The world is not perfect.

If you are a perfectionist, the chances are that almost everything is going to ruin your day because the world and the people in it are not perfect. Imperfection is part of life.

The world is full of blemishes. Even roses have thorns...and mildew...and aphids... And, yet, they are beautiful to look at and sweet to smell.

By the way, have you noticed that the weather isn't always perfect either? We get too much rain, or too little. We get snow when it should be spring. We get hurricanes where they hardly ever happen.

And people aren't perfect either! They don't keep their word or their appointments. They yell when you want quiet or are quiet when you want conversation. They are lazy, sometimes rude, and frequently smelly.

By insisting on perfection, we throw away what we have for something that may be out of reach. We live our lives never being satisfied because there is always something that is not quite right...the car has a slight dent in it...the plane is an hour late...the waiter forgot to bring the salad dressing on the side.

I got into that "perfection trap" soon after I moved to San Francisco. I had come from my hometown, New York City, where I'd attend nearly every musical on Broadway. Then, when I moved to the West Coast, I stopped going to shows because I felt that the actors in the traveling or local productions were never as good as those on the Great White Way.

Broadway does get the cream of the crop talent-wise, but comparing the New York shows to my local productions robbed me of the pleasure I could have gotten from these shows. Seeking perfection is a seldom fulfilling and often a disappointing journey.

Another New York-related story about perfection: When I worked at CBS Television, I had a very strict English boss. He was a stickler for details. When I showed him my drawings for his approval, he would scrutinize every word, then cross every letter "T" I forgot to cross. He also insisted that when his secretary brought him his morning tea and toast that the toast be upright. He would go into a rage if it weren't that way.

I always found it somewhat laughable and a bit absurd to make a fuss over such a minor matter. After all, the toast was still warm. The toast was still very much edible. The toast was still toast.

Consider major league baseball where the "perfect game" has been achieved only twenty-three times. Does that make the thousands of other games less enjoyable or not worth watching?

Or look in the mirror and chances are, like most people, that your face is not perfectly symmetrical. That's what makes it, and you, interesting.

A lot of people get stressed out because of some aspect of themselves that is not perfect. What is looking perfect anyhow? Even the publicity photos of Hollywood stars are touched up. Moreover, it is *not* looking and *not* sounding like everyone else that can be your best asset. Many famous actors and comedians, for example, have distinct looks and characteristics that make them memorable. Think of Jack Nicholson, Carol Channing, or Phyllis Diller.

I, like my father, am nearly bald. I'm not thrilled that I

don't have much hair but that's the way it is. I started losing hair in high school and it never stopped. I have accepted it by using humor to help me deal with how I look. I tell people, "I'm a former expert on how to cure baldness." The self-effacing humor helps me relax about my being follicly challenged and connects me to people who laugh with me, not at me. There is an old adage that if you can laugh at yourself before anyone else does, then you get the upper hand. That is exactly what I am doing when joking about my baldness.

My father, on the other hand, went through life hating the fact that he had very little hair. No one could even mention the obvious in front of him without his becoming defensive and angry.

It's your difference that makes you special, so embrace it. And once you can embrace it, you will be more comfortable about who you are so that you can poke fun and laugh at those things that formerly may have stressed you out, annoyed you, and ruined your day.

Speaking about imperfection, for those who remember the past commercials for Ivory soap, even it was only "$99^{44/100}$% Pure."

~~~~~~~~~~~~~~~~~~~~~~

Gold in the Cracks

When the Japanese mend broken objects, they exaggerate the damage by putting gold in the cracks. They do this because they believe that when something has suffered damage, and has a history, it becomes more beautiful.

Reverend Ken Daigle, the minister at Unity San Francisco, used this as a basis for his congregational talk about the value of imperfections:

"In our society we seem to be always seeking perfection, the perfect outfit, the perfect job, the perfect home, the perfect mate. You get the idea. But in certain cultures imperfections are celebrated. The Navaho, for instance, weave into each rug a thread that appears to be a mistake. Other Native American tribes create a 'flaw' in their pottery. The weaver and potter consider this 'mistake' to be a path for Spirit to enter.

"This is a much more healing and helpful way to look at our all-too-human tendency to make mistakes. When we have the wisdom and compassion to accept our errors and failures, as a path for Spirit to enter, then will we risk more in our work and in our lives? Will we stop worrying about perfection and focus instead on the joy and adventure of life?"

~~~~~~~~~~~~~~~~~~~~~~~~~~~~

Follow-Up

All of us have schnozzles...if not in our faces, then in our character, minds, or habits. When we admit our schnozzle, instead of defending them, we begin to laugh, and the world laughs with us.

—JIMMY DURANTE,
comedian

Is there something in your life that is not quite as perfect as you would like it to be? Something you don't like about the way you look? Something in your surroundings that annoy you because it is not exactly as you think it should be?

Can you embrace those imperfections instead of letting them ruin your day?

This week, start with your own imperfection—things you don't like about your looks or your personality. Once you deal with those, you can then move on to include other non-perfect people who irritate you or those seemingly imperfect things in your surroundings.

Focus on identifying what characteristics you have that make you different from anyone else on this planet. What makes you special? What quirks in your character make you a one-of-a-kind celebrity in your world?

If I listed mine, some of those would be my stubbornness, my bald head, my difficulty walking down stairs, my aging lines on my face, my being an abysmal player in any sport, my taking risks, my overly positive attitude, my being a compulsive planner, etc.

Now make your own list. Then, each day this week, acknowledge and honor one of those attributes that make you special—and perfect.

Lighten-Up

There is a store that sells husbands in New York City. The store has six floors and the value of the products increase as the shopper ascends the flights. The caveat? You are only allowed to shop there once.

The shopper may choose any item from a particular floor, or choose to go up to the next floor, but once you go up, you cannot go back except to exit the building.

So, let's follow a woman as she shops for the first and only time in The Husband Store.

The first floor sign reads: "These men have jobs."

Intrigued, she continues to the second floor, where the sign reads: "These men have jobs and love kids."

She thinks, "That's nice, but I want more."

So she continues upward. The third floor sign reads: "These men have jobs, love kids, and are extremely good looking."

"Wow," she thinks, but feels compelled to keep going. Up on the fourth floor the sign reads: "These men have jobs, love kids, are drop-dead good looking, and help with housework."

"Amazing!" she exclaims, "I can hardly stand it." Still, she continues to the fifth floor where the sign reads: "These men have jobs, love kids, are drop-dead gorgeous, help with housework, and are great lovers."

She is tempted to stay, but goes to the sixth floor anyway, where the sign reads: "You are visitor number 35,674,923 to this floor. There are no men on this floor. It exists as proof you are impossible to please. Thank you for shopping at The Husband Store."

By the way, to avoid gender bias, the store's owner opened The Wife Store just across the street.

GIVE WHAT YOU WANT TO GET BACK

⌘

*Love only grows by sharing. You can only have more
for yourself by giving it away to others.*

—BRIAN TRACY,
motivational speaker and author

THINK OF A rock thrown into a lake. As soon as it hits, the water ripples radiate out in expanding circles. Your actions are like ripples that extend out into the world. What you say and how you treat people has the potential to radically change everyone with whom you come in contact.

I noticed this concept the other day at the airport. I had just gone through security, as did the couple in front of me. The woman stopped to put her shoes back on just as a man passing behind her slightly bumped into the backpack she was carrying. As he did, he said, "Excuse me," and proceeded on. The woman's companion blared out, "Hey, watch where you are going." The other man reiterated that he said excuse me but that wasn't good enough for the woman's fellow traveler. He escalated the encounter berating, shouting, and cursing the other man.

I was amazed how such a simple innocent occurrence could turn into such a big deal that probably influenced the tone of all three travelers that day.

Did you say an unkind word to someone today? Were you gruff with someone this week? Did you blurt out something that hurt someone recently? The words you speak, and the actions you take, are like pebbles tossed into a lake. Without you even giving much thought to what you say or do, the ripples from your words and actions travel across the sea of humanity. Have you ever noticed, for example, that when you get angry and yell at someone that most of the time they will yell back at you? Or, when you smile at someone, they smile too?

A simple and powerful principle is taking place when things like that occur. That idea is: Whatever you give to the world, the world gives back to you. This is an important concept. It also connects to the notion that nobody can ruin your day. I need to repeat it again: Whatever you give to the world, the world gives back to you.

In keeping with that thought, if you want more happiness in your life, then do something that will make someone else happy. Want more abundance in your life? Then be generous with others. Want to forgive someone? Then forgive yourself first.

It's somewhat paradoxical that when we give, we receive. But it is true. The Bible tells us—"Give, and it will be given to you." St. Francis of Assisi also reminds us, "For it is in giving that we receive." And, scientific studies even prove it. Researchers, for example, found that people who volunteer live longer. And, according to one Syracuse University study, those who donate to charity are forty-two percent happier than non-givers.

I personally experienced the extreme joy of giving a few years ago when a friend, who was also a distant relative, left me a substantial amount of money. I regularly tithe ten percent of all my income to my spiritual home, Unity San Francisco. But I procrastinated for a long time about writing out the large four-figure check. My mind was giving me a lot of resistance. I was thinking about everything I could do with the money instead of giving it away: fly first class to Europe; upgrade my computer; buy a couple of custom-made suits.

In spite of those thoughts, I finished writing the check and reluctantly took it to Unity that Sunday. When the offering basket came closer, my heart began to beat faster and my thoughts began to consider not putting the check in it. I even considered tearing up the check and writing another one for half the amount. After all, I would still be giving away a substantial amount of money. And who would know, anyway?

Then the dreaded decision time came. The basket got closer and closer. When it reached me, I dropped the check in.

Suddenly, and with great surprise to me, instead of what I thought would be a feeling of loss, I felt euphoric. A strong physical sense of joy rushed over me. I was thrilled realizing how fortunate I was to be able to give away such a great sum of money. Instead of feeling poor, I felt rich and overwhelmingly happy.

So if every action has a reaction, then we must be constantly aware of what we are giving to the world if we don't want anyone to ruin our day.

Does It Serve You?

The words below are reportedly inscribed on the wall of Mother Teresa's home in Calcutta. They were taken from an earlier, slightly different version, titled "The Paradoxical Commandments," which was written by nineteen-year-old Kent M. Keith as part of a book for student leaders at Harvard College. They have since been reprinted in numerous versions and in many publications.

"People are often unreasonable, illogical, and self-centered;
    Forgive them anyway.

If you are kind, people may accuse you of selfish, ulterior motives;

Be kind anyway.

If you are successful, you will win some false friends and some true enemies;

Succeed anyway.

If you are honest and frank, people may cheat you;

Be honest and frank anyway.

What you spend years building, someone could destroy overnight;

Build anyway.

If you find serenity and happiness, they may be jealous;

Be happy anyway.

The good you do today, people will often forget tomorrow;

Do good anyway.

Give the world the best you have, and it may never be enough;

Give the world the best you've got anyway.

You see, in the final analysis, it is between you and your God;

It was never between you and them anyway."

—Mother Teresa, Roman Catholic nun

Perhaps it doesn't matter which version you read. What is important is the message. It talks about how people may, among other things, be unreasonable, cheat you, not acknowledge you, be unfriendly, or destroy what you have taken years to build. The advice suggests that when a thing like that happens to you, forgive, be kind, and love those people anyway.

It is great advice but not easy to be kind to people that are pushing your buttons. I'd therefore like to suggest one simple question you can ask yourself when people irritate you and their actions cause you to respond in a negative way. When people upset you, ask yourself: "Does my reaction serve me?"

"Does it serve me to get angry, yell, scream, or carry on?" Or, "Does it serve me to be rude, impolite, and bad-mannered?"

Chances are it doesn't serve you to do any of those things. But being kinder to them might serve you as well as them.

Uncontrolled explosive anger, after all, can spiral out of control and not only ruin your day, but your relationships and your health as well. As Buddha tells us, "Holding on to anger is like grasping a hot coal with the intent of throwing it at someone else; you are the one who gets burned."

And, since we often get back what we give, if we are rude to someone, even if they are rude to us first, it only perpetuates the exchange. Don't believe me? Then watch how easily a few words between two angry people can quickly escalate and grow into a fistfight. "Emotions are contagious," says psychologist Daniel Goleman. "You know after you have a really fun coffee date with a friend, you feel good. When you have a rude clerk in a store, you walk away feeling bad."

~~~~~~~~~~~~~~~~~~~~~~~~~~

Follow-Up

As we work to create light for others, we naturally light our own way.

—MARY ANNE RADMACHER, *author and artist*

Two years ago, I received a letter from a young woman at college who was inspired by my work of bringing joy to people. She told me that, in a similar vein, her passion was to make people's day. She gave me some wonderful examples of this. Among others, she gives out free hugs, sends handwritten anonymous thank-you cards, hides positive affirmations in public places, and asks people what was the best part of their day. The college student didn't reveal what she received in return for her spreading joy but I could tell from the look and tone of the letter that she is well on her way to uplifting people when the world is getting them down.

As you go through your day, notice what you are putting out in the world. Notice how people react to what you are giving to them. Also notice what you are getting back.

If what you get back is not what you want, then consider Steve Maraboli's advice. In his book, *Unapologetically You*, he says, "Don't wait for other people to be loving, giving, compassionate, grateful, forgiving, generous, or friendly... lead the way!"

No matter what the situation, you can lead the way and change how you react to people or situations. In your encounters today, can you: Add a smile? Use some kinder words? Do what you are doing with more love and compassion?

Lighten-Up

Humorist Art Buchwald beautifully illustrates this wake-up call with a realization he had while riding in a taxicab:

I was in New York the other day and rode with a friend in a taxi. When we got out, my friend said to the driver, "Thank you for the ride. You did a superb job of driving."

The taxi driver was stunned for a second. Then he said, "Are you a wise guy or something?"

"No, my dear man. I'm not putting you on. I admire the way you keep cool in heavy traffic."

"Yeah," the driver said and drove off.

"What was that all about?" I asked.

"I'm trying to bring love back to New York," he said. "I believe it's the only thing that can save the city."

"How can one man save the city?"

"It's not one man. I believe I made the taxi driver's day. Suppose he has twenty fares. He's going to be nice to those twenty fares because someone was nice to him. Those fares in turn will be kinder to their employees, or shopkeepers, or waiters, or even their own families. Eventually the goodwill could spread to at least a thousand people. Now, that isn't bad, is it?"

"But you're depending on that taxi driver to pass your goodwill to others."

"I'm not depending on it," my friend said, "I'm aware that the system isn't foolproof, so I might deal with ten different people today. If, out of ten, I can make three happy, then eventually I can indirectly influence the attitudes of three thousand more."

"It sounds good on paper," I admitted, "but I'm not sure it works in practice."

"Nothing is lost if it doesn't. It didn't take any of my time to tell that man he was doing a good job. He received neither a larger tip nor a smaller tip. If it fell on deaf ears, so what? Tomorrow there will be another taxi driver whom I can try to make happy..."

WATCH OUT FOR TRAFFIC JAMS

⌘

If you are distressed by anything external, the pain is not due to the thing itself but to your own estimate of it; and this you have the power to revoke at any moment.

—MARCUS AURELIUS,
Roman emperor

LIFE IS FILLED with traffic jams. Not only on the highway where cars are but also on the highway of life, where we travel daily. We go along and everything is fine, then we dent the car, our child breaks their arm, we don't get the raise we were promised, our flight is cancelled, we are told we have a serious illness, etc.

Some are minor stop-then-go places that may slow us

down for a short time, and others are major traffic jams that stop us in our tracks. All of these stuck places, whether minor or major, are chances for us to notice how we react to them.

A friend of mine, for example, has cancer. Almost daily, she posts her progress and her feelings about her treatments online. Here is what she wrote one day:

"I woke up thinking about how I often say that this cancer is a blip on the screen, but it's actually more like a little standstill on the highway. Let me make some analogous statements here.

"You know how you can be watching TV and the picture goes out or there's interference or cable goes out or something? You can know that it might be only momentary, but when it drags on, it's annoying. You miss the rest of the show you were watching and are left hanging. You get on the call to the cable company only to wait. Or, when you're driving down the road and all of a sudden traffic comes to an abrupt stop...or maybe even creeps, but very slowly. You are still delayed, and often for a long time.

"Well, having this cancer is sort of like these things. I know it will end...eventually, but it is definitely an interruption in my life, in many, many ways."

My friend made the choice to do what she had to do medically to rid herself of the cancer and to continue to live her life as fully as her strength allowed. Her traffic jam has eased up and she has now moved on with her life.

I ♥ Traffic Jams

On a fairly good day, I spend two hours a day com-
muting by car from home to work and back. "So
what do you do?" asked a colleague, when she
learned that I drive daily. I smiled benignly, for she
might be amazed if I listed all the things I did during
traffic jams. She might even think me crazy if I told
her I simply love traffic jams.

Didn't someone say, "Learn to accept the things
you cannot change?" I began to do just that, out of
sheer survival instinct. For starters, I became immune
to jeers and rude comments from co-road users who
would sometimes spit out expletives from their car
windows. The immunity buildup was greatly aided
by the acquisition of an air-conditioned car that
effectively shut out the noise. I could simply enjoy
the radio or recorded music, if I was in the mood.

Reading is something you can do effortlessly
while stuck in traffic. You might want to have a book-
mark when traffic moves. Hopefully the book is not
an engrossing thriller that will inure you to your surroundings—unless you want a dozen people honk-
ing behind you when the light turns green! I do take
a sheet or two of the day's newspaper to complete
reading pieces I didn't have time to finish at home.

I know of some who chant mantras at traffic
jams...or knit...but since I do neither, my favored

time-pass is reading, which is why I have come to love traffic jams. How else does one make the time to read stuff that has nothing to do with your work or children?

The other day I was in the middle of a beautiful short story. I had just a paragraph left and was praying that the light wouldn't turn green until I finished the last line! And the traffic-god did heed my request.

—Narayani Ganesh,
The Times of India (paraphrased)

~~~~~~~~~~~~~~~~~~~~~~~~~~

Follow-Up

If all the cars in the United States were placed end to end, it would probably be Labor Day weekend.

—DOUG LARSON,
columnist

Were you stuck in a traffic jam this week, either on the highway or elsewhere? Were you able to react to it differently than you have in the past, perhaps in a more positive way?

If not, realize that the unpleasant things you are experiencing right now, or have encountered this week, are minor stop-and-go places in life's big picture. Traffic jams are only temporary bottlenecks; they eventually clear up and resolve themselves.

Remember, nothing lasts. This too shall pass.

P.S.: Caught in an actual traffic jam on the highway? Here are a few fun things you can do while you wait: Sing as loud as you want, with or without the radio. Guess what people in other cars do for a living, or how old they are. Keep a jar of bubbles in the car and blow bubbles out the window.

Lighten-Up

One day, as I was waiting in a long line at a toll plaza on the San Francisco–Oakland Bay Bridge, a black stretch limo pulled up beside my car. As I am prone to do when I'm stuck in a traffic jam, I rolled down the window and blew bubbles out my window. When the passenger in the backseat of the limo saw the bubbles, she rolled down her window and shouted, "Blow some my way." Noticing that she was sipping champagne in the backseat, I shouted back, "Throw some bubbly my way." We both had a good laugh as the traffic eased up and we proceeded to the tollbooth.

REFRAME TO REMAIN SANE

⌘

In the scheme of things, what you do and whether you are angry or not will have all the impact of another glass of water being thrown over Niagara Falls. Whether you choose laughter or anger will not matter much—except that the former will fill your present moments with happiness, and the latter will waste them in misery.

—WAYNE DYER,
author and self-help advocate

TWO SALESMEN WORKED for competing shoe companies. Both were sent to a remote part of the world where neither company had any salespeople. When they arrived they both realized that this territory was unlike any they had ever seen before. The people in the region went barefoot all the time. No one wore any shoes.

As soon as the salesmen realized the situation both sent their home office a message to inform them of the situation. Their messages, however, were quite different.

One salesman's message read: "Don't send any more shoes. No one here wears any."

The other message said: "Send all the shoes you can. No one here has any."

Both men experienced the same situation yet each reacted in a totally different way—two different reactions to the same situation. Each interpreted the incident differently. So it is not the event that can ruin your day, it is how you react to it.

In other words, we create our own reality. You see your experience one way but someone else might see it differently. In actuality, things are the way they are. We are the ones who give them meaning. When someone else's behavior, or some situation triggers a negative response from you, you can take that negative situation and reframe it to a more positive one.

In her book, *Magnificent...Married or Not*, author Cloris Kylie suggests that those who feel victimized due to a divorce replace their negative statements with those that reflect their divine nature. For example, reframe "I am defeated" to "I am learning and growing." Reframe "I am angry" to "I am forgiving." Reframe "I am demanding justice" to "I am giving."

Salespeople often use the technique of replacing negative outcomes with a more positive outlook when encountering one rejection after another. They frequently remind themselves when someone doesn't buy their product, they haven't really lost a sale; they are merely one step closer to getting one. Similarly, when a meeting planner tells me that they have selected someone other than me to be their keynote speaker, yes, it is disappointing but I reframe it. It gives me more time to write my next book.

Another example in reframing occurred with my new six-month-old puppy. One day I walked into the kitchen and found her chewing on my reading glasses. There were five or six toys, several chew sticks, and a bone or two surrounding her, yet there she was demolishing my glasses.

At first, I got upset. But then, seeing the plethora of "goodies" around her, I began to focus on what an abundant world we live in, including my having such a cute, playful puppy. That simple reframing helped me appreciate the dog instead of being upset with her.

You too can get one step closer to having a great day, every day, by reframing your upsets. Often a small shift in your focus can lead you to a big shift of perception.

~~~~~~~~~~~~~~~~~~~~~~~~~~~~

Hard to Tell

"Several summers ago I spent three days on a barrier island where loggerhead turtles were laying their eggs. One night while the tide was out, I watched a huge female heave herself up on the beach and dig her nest and empty her eggs into it. Afraid of disturbing her, I left before she was finished. The next morning I returned to see if I could find the spot where her eggs lay hidden in the sand. What I found were her tracks leading in the wrong direction. Instead of heading back out to sea, she had wandered into the dunes, which were already as hot as asphalt in the morning sun.

"A little ways inland I found her: Exhausted, all but baked, her head and flippers caked with dried sand. After pouring water on her and covering her with sea oats, I fetched a park ranger who returned with a jeep to rescue her. He flipped her on her back, strapped tire chains around her front legs, and hooked the chains to a trailer hitch on his jeep. Then I watched horrified as he took off, yanking her body forward so that her mouth filled with sand and her neck bent so far back I thought it would break.

"The ranger hauled her over the dunes and down onto the beach. At the ocean's edge, he unhooked her and turned her right side up. She lay motionless in the surf as the water lapped at her body; washing

135

the sand from her eyes and making her skin shine again. A wave broke over her; she lifted her head slightly, moving her back legs. Other waves brought her further back to life until one of them made her light enough to find a foothold and push off, back into the ocean.

"Watching her swim slowly away and remembering her nightmare ride through the dunes, I reflected that it is sometimes hard to tell whether you are being killed or saved by the hands that turn your life upside down."

—Barbara Brown Taylor,
The Other Side magazine, March/April 2000

Follow-Up

My life has been filled with terrible misfortunes most of which have never happened.

—MICHEL DE MONTAIGNE,
French writer

Today, take something crappy that happened and reframe it into something happier. If a coworker is rude or disrespectful, if your boss makes you angry with unreasonable demands, if you are having an argument with your spouse, ask yourself one or more of these questions:

Does getting upset or angry serve me?

Does being upset or angry contribute to my well-being?

Does being upset or angry bring me more or less joy into my life?

What am I making this mean?

What can I learn from being upset or angry?

Lighten-Up

A man and woman had been married for more than fifty years. They kept no secrets from each other except that the woman had a shoebox in the top of her closet that she had cautioned her husband never to open or ask her about.

For all of these years, he never thought about the box, but one day the woman got sick and the doctor said she would not recover.

In trying to sort out their affairs, the man took down the shoebox and brought it to his wife's bedside. She agreed that it was time that he should know what was in the box. When he opened it, he found two crocheted dolls and $95,000 in cash.

He asked her about the contents.

"When we were to be married," she said, "my grandmother told me the secret of a happy marriage was to never argue. She told me that if I ever got angry with you, I should just keep quiet and crochet a doll."

The man was so moved; he had to fight back tears. Only two precious dolls were in the box. She had only been angry with him two times in all those years.

"Honey," he said, "that explains the dolls, but what about all of this money? Where did it come from?"

"Oh," she said, "that's the money I made from selling the dolls."

TAP INTO THE POWER OF WORDS

⌘

*Anxiety weighs down the human heart,
but a good word cheers it up.*

—PROVERBS 12:25

AS I WRITE this book, there is a big controversy about whether or not the violence depicted on TV and in video games is responsible for the recent killing of twenty students who were shot by another student. Makers of those violent video games and producers defend themselves by saying the shooting and killings in their productions are not real. They claim they produce only a script, someone is only acting out a part.

That is true, it's not real; it's only actors. But when we see people being shot and killed day after day on TV, in movies, in video games, or hear about real live people being killed on the nightly news, it has to influence us. As one psychologist noted, "It desensitizes us and in a sense dehumanizes us." In other words, the visuals we see and the words we constantly hear changes the way we perceive things.

Moreover, studies have shown that young children don't understand the finality of death. They destroy one of their toys, for example, and suddenly another one is bought to replace it. Or they see an actor on TV shot to death only to see him alive again on another show.

Interestingly, the newspaper article I read about violence in films and on TV was on the same page with a comment by actor James Marsden. Noting what a great job his TV wife on *30 Rock* was doing as host of the Golden Globe Awards, Marsden commented, "It was nice to see my bride up on stage *killing* it."

Words and images have a significant influence on us, even to the point of changing our bodily reactions. Give people a drink of orange juice, for example, and tell them that there is vodka in it, and at least half of them say they felt intoxicated. Other experiments, one dealing with sleep and one with stress, have also come to the same conclusion—your body acts according to what you have been told or what you thought was happening, even when it wasn't the case. Moreover, recent research is showing that it is not merely stress that can be harmful but that stressing out about stress can kill you even quicker.

Most of us have heard about the effect of placebos—

patients in clinical trials who improve thinking they were getting real medication when they were only given a sugar pill. But what science is also finding is that the same mind-body connection that can heal can also harm. This "nocebo effect" has been demonstrated in a number of studies.

For example, when a patient was told that they might experience nausea, they felt nauseous. If the doctor suggested they might get a headache from the prescribed medicine, they did. And patients given a saline solution but thought it was chemotherapy reacted the same way many chemo patients do; they threw up or lost their hair.

Nocebos can even be a matter of life and death. Women who believed they were predisposed to heart disease had a greater chance of dying from it. In addition, patients who were about to have surgery, and convinced of their impending death, usually died, whereas as those who were merely apprehensive about death, did not.

I personally saw the effect of nocebos when my wife was seriously ill. The doctor told her she had three years to live. She died three years later. Would she have lived longer if he hadn't specified a time or if he said that she would live for five or ten years? Who knows? But what we do know, and what science is proving, is that we need to watch what we view, watch what we think, and watch what we say.

~~~~~~~~~~~~~~~~~~~~~~~~~~~~

Words and Water

Masaru Emoto is a researcher from Japan whose experiments became widely known when they were featured in the film *What the Bleep Do We Know!?* and in his book *The Hidden Messages in Water*. What Emoto discovered is that molecules in water can be affected by our thoughts, feelings, and words. He found that water that was exposed to loving words showed brilliant and colorful snowflake patterns. Water exposed to negative thoughts, on the other hand, formed incomplete, asymmetrical patterns with dull colors.

Since our bodies are made up of around sixty percent water, the implication of this experiment is vast. It indicates that what thoughts we are having and the words we are using could have a major impact on our physical reality.

In another experiment along these lines, Emoto put some cooked rice into two containers. On one container he wrote "thank you" and on the other "you fool." Then he instructed schoolchildren to say the words on the jars out loud as they passed them every day. At the end of thirty days, the rice in the container with "thank you" on it had barely changed, while the rice inside the "you fool" jar was moldy and rotten.

Some people question the results of these

studies, especially the latter one. Still, when you think about people who have been healed by prayers, or the scientific studies showing the connection between mind and body, the power of words makes a lot of sense.

~~~~~~~~~~~~~~~~~~~~~~

Follow-Up

Select your thoughts just the same way you select your clothes every day. This is a power you can cultivate. If you want to control things in your life, work on the mind. That's the only thing you should be trying to control.

—ELIZABETH GILBERT,
author

When you wake up tomorrow, and every day for the rest of the week, try starting your day with a word or phrase that is positive, uplifting, or inspiring.

Why start your day that way? Because, as Billie Freeman wrote in an article on the Unity website, "When your words are constructive, you find that your reaction to them is constructive. If throughout the day you express only positive ideas through good words, the end of the day will find you feeling unsurpassably content."

So if you want to have a great day, today, and every day, and not have anyone ruin it, you can do two simple things: 1) Begin your day with a positive word or two; and 2) Take a suggestion from author Steve Maraboli and ask yourself, "How would your life be different if...you stopped allowing other people to dilute or poison your day with their words or opinions?"

Lighten-Up

"I was going through airport security the other month, participating in the grind of pulling out my laptop and my baggie full of plastic bottles, and removing my belt and my shoes and my watch and my jacket and trying to fit them all into the plastic bin in such a way that nothing would fall out as it went through its screening.

"On the other side, I quickly gathered my belongings so they wouldn't get run over by the oncoming stream of objects. I started shuffling forward with my shoes half on and my arms weighed down by my scattering of possessions. As I glanced up, I saw a group of chairs and tables with an accompanying sign that read: 'Recombobulation Area.'

"'Ha!' I grunted with laughter and relief. 'How perfect is that!'

"Not only did I appreciate having some space to pull myself together, but even more so, I loved that someone had invented this word and had gone to the effort of naming this area—I loved how it created a moment of unexpected lightness, especially when I was feeling a bit bogged down."

—KAREN HORNEFFER-GINTER,
psychologist and author

WATCH WHAT YOU TELL YOURSELF

⌘

Like food is to the body, self-talk is to the mind. Don't let any junk thoughts repeat in your head.

—MADDY MALHOTRA,
author/speaker

WORDS AND IMAGES that surround us, as well as what we say to other people, are important ingredients that influence what kind of day we have. But perhaps the most important influence of our day is what we say to ourselves—our self-talk. If you want to have a great day, every day, start noticing your thoughts and how many times they are not so positive. In fact, a great deal of the time, they are probably negative.

I recently read two things that might indicate why we are

prone toward leaning to the negative rather than the positive. The first is something that stems from caveman times when we had to be on a constant lookout for things that might harm us such as caves collapsing, animals attacking, or landslides occurring. So, instead of focusing on the good things that might have surrounded them, the cavemen, in order to protect themselves, focused on the bad things that might happen. Some vestiges of that, apparently, still remain.

The second comes from studies done with adults and children. What the studies found was that for every one positive thing an adult says to a child, they say twelve negative things.

Often advice like "You shouldn't..." "Don't do that..." "Sit down and shut up..." comes rolling out of a parent's mouth without their even realizing it. So the child is constantly hearing negative commands that will go on to color their adult life. Parents need to be constantly aware and more conscious of what they tell their children.

When my daughter was growing up, I had the image of her being like a sponge. She would soak in everything I said one day and it would come back to me sometime in the future.

My spouse has a wonderful example of that. It took place between his mother and her grandchildren. They were visiting her and, at one point, started fighting while playing. Her grandson screamed at his sister, "I'll kill you. I'll kill you." Finding this very upsetting, especially coming from a seven-year-old, she scolded, "That's terrible. Where did you hear such an awful thing?" He replied, "From you, Grandma."

If we are to counteract our supposed predisposition to negativity, another thing to remember is that we no longer live in caves; most of the time we are safe.

So instead of focusing our energy on things that might harm us, or constantly bombarding our kids with negative warnings, we need to focus on more positive things, things that will nurture us and help us, and help our children grow mentally and spiritually. That is where affirmations come in. Whether you call them prayers, intentions, mantras, meditations, or even resolutions, they can help remind you what you want in any situation.

According to several studies, positive self-talk can improve how we handle challenging circumstances. One study, for example, found that college students who paused at the start of an argument to focus on affirmations unrelated to the argument were less likely to escalate the fight.

Another study found that when female students wrote affirmations to themselves in an introductory physics class, their test scores improved.

And many top athletes visualize and affirm their achievement before attempting it. As Gayle Davis, a sports psychologist who works with Olympic athletes, notes, "Your mind believes what you put in it."

In my workshops, I show two lists on the PowerPoint. One list has only positive words, such as joy, happy, cheerful, etc. The other list has only negative words, such as despair, hopeless, misery, etc.

In part of the exercise, I ask participants to read in unison each list out loud. Then I ask them how they felt reading the positive and negative lists. Their response is, as expected, that one list brought them down while the other lifted them up.

Our mind cannot hold both negative and positive thoughts at the same time. Without realizing it, we are feeding our brain either positive thoughts or negative ones with every word we use. Every millisecond of the day, we are unconsciously deciding what kind of day we are creating.

Perhaps it is time to be more conscious of what we think and what we say since words can give us hope and help us heal. They also can bring hurt and heartache. Words can poison our thoughts or give them power. Tap into their positive power now.

~~~~~~~~~~~~~~~~~~~~~~~~~~~~~~

A Matter of Life and Death

Robert Desnos was a surrealist poet who was captured by the Nazis and imprisoned in a death camp for being a member of the French Resistance during World War II. Writer Susan Griffin detailed his amazing story (*The Whole Earth Review,* Spring 1996) of how he saved lives merely by what he told the doomed prisoners:

"One day Desnos and others were taken away from their barracks. The prisoners rode on the back of a flatbed truck; they knew the truck was going to the gas chamber; no one spoke. Soon they arrived and the guards ordered them off the truck. When they began to move toward the gas chamber, suddenly Desnos jumped out of line and grabbed the hand of the woman in front of him. He was animated and he began to read her palm. The forecast was good: a long life, many grandchildren, abundant joy. A person nearby offered his palm to Desnos. Here, too, Desnos foresaw a long life filled with happiness and success. The other prisoners came to life, eagerly thrusting their palms toward Desnos and, in each case, he foresaw long and joyous lives.

"The guards became visibly disoriented. Minutes before they were on a routine mission, the outcome of which seemed inevitable, but now they became tentative in their movements. Desnos was so effective in creating a new reality that the guards were unable to go through with the executions. They ordered the prisoners back onto the truck and took them back to the barracks. Desnos never was executed. Through the power of imagination, he saved his own life and the lives of others."

~~~~~~~~~~~~~~~~~~~~~~~~~~~~

Follow-Up

*We cannot always control our thoughts, but we can
control our words, and repetition impresses the
subconscious, and we are then
master of the situation.*

—FLORENCE SCOVEL SHINN,
spiritual teacher and artist

Scott Adams was a young middle manager that dreamed of being a famous cartoonist one day. In addition to sending out packets of cartoons about the corporate world, he also wrote down the words "I will become a syndicated columnist" fifteen times a day, every day. Adams has had two cartoon books on the *New York Times* bestseller list and his cartoons are syndicated worldwide. With affirmations, notes Adams, "there are no harmful side effects and they do help focus your energy."

With our natural bias toward the negative and all the negative news fed to us every hour by the media, it may take an extra effort to refocus our thoughts. That is where affirmations, the process of repeating positive statements, can come in handy.

As you saw in a previous section of the book, where I talk about finding the perfect publisher, I am a firm believer in affirmations. So to help you have a great day by eliminating negative thinking and reinforcing the positive in your life, below are some affirmations you might try. And if these don't call out to you, then simply make up your own. Remember that their power lies in repeating them often or constantly surrounding yourself with them.

"I let go so I can see clearly."

"I choose to find optimistic ways to look at my circumstance."

"I surround myself with love, hope, and compassion."

"I take comfort in knowing I can always step away from a situation."

"The past has no hold over me anymore."

"I only attract positive people in my life."

"Everything is going to work out for the highest good."

Or you can borrow some from these self-help authors:

"The more I focus my mind upon the good, the more good comes to me."— Louise Hay

"Luminous and productive energy flows through me." —Marianne Mitchell

"My inner guidance is there for me to call on anytime I need or want extra clarity, wisdom, knowledge, support, creative inspiration, love, or companionship."—Shakti Gawain

"I change my life by transforming myself."—Amy Zerner and Monte Faber

"That which I create in the world returns to me."—Pamela Wells

One other thing about affirmations—a friend of mine told me that she sings hers. She says it is not only more playful but it also helps her overcome any resistance to what she is trying to achieve. Try it.

Lighten-Up

In his book, *Duck Soup for the Soul,* author Swami Beyondananda (aka Steve Bhaerman), lists some humorous affirmations to help you "attune your own karma." First, among others, he suggests these to help you relax: Put your karma into park. Turn off your ignition. Let all exhaustion escape from your tailpipe.

Then he suggests that you repeat the following playful affirmations:

"My battery is fully charged and I am getting plenty of juice."

"My front end is aligned with perfection."

"I cruise easily with the flow of traffic, and experience no delays."

TELL THE TRUTH

⌘

The whole universe depends on everything fitting
together just right. If one piece busts, even the
smallest piece...the whole universe will get busted.

—HUSHPUPPY,
in the movie *Beasts of the Southern Wild*

ONE MORE THING about the power of words—don't
lie. Why? In my opinion, lying upsets the fabric of the
universe.

Lies might help you feel better today but down the road,
lies can come back to haunt you. If you doubt that, look
at some of the current politicians or athletes in the news.
They deny their actions and then, when it finally comes out
that they did what they said they didn't do, they sheepishly

apologize. But it is too late; they have lost trust with their fans and the public.

Once someone finds out you lied, it creates mistrust between you and the other person. In addition, it's more work to lie than to tell the truth. From the moment you lie, you have got to keep everything in order. You have got to remember everything you said so that you don't contradict yourself down the road.

When my daughter was young, she once lied to me about some small matter. I told her never to lie to me again because once she did I could never trust anything she told me. I told her that I may not like what she said, but I'd rather she tell me the truth and we deal with whatever it is she did.

Lance Armstrong, the cyclist and winner of seven Tour de France titles, admitted that he took performance-enhancing drugs. For years, he denied the fact. But, perhaps even more disturbing, he fought his accusers and destroyed their careers by disavowing their accusations. Many supporters of Armstrong defended him, pointing out his icon status with the cancer community and millions of dollars he raised for research. All that is true, but his good work and image is forever tarnished by his gross lies.

In the end, lying ruined Armstrong's career. Lying could ruin yours too. I think eventually our lies eat away at us. At the very least they have the potential to make us feel uncomfortable. It is probably why Armstrong finally confessed. At some point, when the lies get too big, you need, as he did, to set things right.

Years ago, when there was a less open climate toward gay people, I lied to one meeting planner when she asked whether I ever got married again after my wife died.

I lied and said, "I did."

Then she asked what my wife's name was.

Since I didn't want to reveal that I was a gay man in a long-term relationship with another man, I made up a woman's name. "Elizabeth," I said.

Then she asked what my wife did.

I lied again and said "she" was a therapist, which was the profession of my male partner.

The conversation went on like that as I got deeper and deeper into lying. It finally ended when she dropped me off at the hotel.

The minute I closed the car door, I felt awful. The meeting planner had gone out of her way to hire me to speak at her church. She was most gracious and treated me like royalty. And here I was not telling her the truth.

For over an hour, I agonized about what I did. And what I could do to right that. The lies weighed me down. Finally, in order to set the record straight and undo the burden I felt, I picked up the phone and called her.

"I lied to you," I said.

She had no idea what I was talking about until I explained what I lied about.

She was very forgiving. As a result of my sharing who I really was, we have kept in touch for more than eighteen years and have become good friends. In fact, last year when her husband died, I flew to San Diego to be part of his memorial service.

Follow-Up

Integrity is the condition in which the life you are living in the outer world matches who you are in the inner world.

—ALAN COHEN,
author

The word "integrity" comes from the Latin word *integritas*, which means wholeness. So when you are lying, you are not telling the whole truth, you are not complete, you are not whole.

Some of the small things you can do to boost your integrity and your truthfulness are: Refrain from telling small white lies or insincere compliments. If you do catch yourself being insincere or telling a white lie, admit it to yourself and to the other person.

For a week, keep a "Lie List" handy and at the end of each day write down any non-truths you may have told. See if you can make the list shorter each day. Part of coming from a place of integrity means admitting that you lied. See if you can do that. And once you do admit that you lied, remember to apologize.

Lighten-Up

A woman confesses to a priest that she has told a malicious lie about another person.

"Well," says the priest, "here is your penance. Go to the top of your building with a feather pillow, slit it open, and throw all the feathers into the wind."

The next week the woman returns to the confessional.

"Did you do what I asked?" says the priest.

"Yes," she says.

"Now," he says, "go back and pick up all the feathers."

"Oh, but I can't," she says. "By now they're everywhere!"

"And so are your lies," says the priest.

TAKE A VACATION

⌘

A vacation is having nothing to do
and all day to do it in.

—ROBERT ORBEN,
comedy writer

WE ARE ABOUT halfway through the book. Perhaps it is time to take a break. We all need to take a vacation from time to time to assess where we are, to process what we have learned, and to take a deep breath before we continue on our journey.

Now is the time to do that.

~~~~~~~~~~~~~~~~~~~~~~~~~~~~~~

Time Out

Often we feel that we don't have time to take a break and take a vacation. But time away is important for both health and longevity. The Global Coalition on Aging, for example, says, "women who vacationed at least twice a year had significantly lower risk for heart issues and death than women who vacationed every six years." Getting away is also vital to men. According to the Coalition, "Men who took annual vacations lowered the risk of death from heart disease by thirty percent over the non-vacationing group."

~~~~~~~~~~~~~~~~~~~~~~~~~~~~~~

Follow-Up

The alternative to a vacation is to stay home and tip every third person you see.

—ANONYMOUS

Take time off this week. Take a break. Take a trip. "Take a schvitz" (a Woody Allen line from his play *Death Knocks*)... or, do nothing.

Lighten-Up

Babies don't need a vacation, but I still see them at the beach...it pisses me off! I'll go over to a little baby and say, "What are you doing here? You haven't worked a day in your life!"

—STEVEN WRIGHT,
comedian

BE GRATEFUL

⌘

*Gratitude unlocks the fullness of life. It turns what
we have into enough, and more. It turns denial into
acceptance, chaos to order, confusion to clarity. It
can turn a meal into a feast, a house into a home, a
stranger into a friend.*

—MELODY BEATTIE,
author

FOUR CENTS ON the street in Las Vegas
Delicious dinner prepared by my nephew Justin
$30 on Haight Street
$3,400 from the U.S. Treasury for over-payment of taxes
Invited to a wonderful party
Found three cents on the street

Cookies from the neighbor
Open seat next to me on my flight from JFK to SFO
Free ticket to the International Film Festival
$1.13 on the street in three different places
A penny and a dime on the street, today, the day I'm writing this.

The above list contains just a few of the items from my personal gratitude journal. It consists of money and other things that have appeared in my life. They happen on a regular basis and I am grateful for them. So I write them down and say "Thank You" for all of the riches that come into my life, no matter how small.

Last year, mostly walking the dog, my spouse and I found a total of $28.55, or nearly eight cents a day. We bless the money at the end of the year and give the dollar bills to the homeless and the pennies to a charity called Every Penny Counts.

I have a lot of prosperity in my life, not only in the money I find on the street but also in the wonderful friends and family I have and in having a profession that both nurtures others and me. Because of all that, a friend of mine says that I live a charmed life. Maybe so, maybe not. As you read earlier, I'm a firm believer in affirmations. The one I use to support my so-called "charmed life," and you are welcome to borrow it if you like, is, "The World Treats Me as Royalty Wherever I Go." The interesting thing about repeating that affirmation to myself is that because I expect that to happen, it often does.

Equally as powerful as affirmations is what I've discovered about gratitude. The more I am grateful when the world treats me as royalty, the more great things come into my life. I'm not sure exactly why this happens but perhaps Ralph Marston, of the website The Daily Motivator®, has a clue. He asks, "What if you gave someone a gift, and they neglected to thank you for it—would you be likely to give them another? Life is the same way. In order to attract more of the blessings that life has to offer, you must truly appreciate what you already have."

Irish actress and songwriter, Andrea Corr, further expands on this. She says, "Of course there are bad people in the world. Good, bad, it happens unfortunately. But in a way I think if there was more focus on the good, more good would happen."

A colleague of mine, author and spiritual teacher Pragito Dove, carries this idea one step further. She says, "It is in *your* best interest to find a way to be grateful to all people—yes, even if you hate them, even if they drive you crazy, even if you are completely justified in hating them because of their unspeakably heinous behavior toward you."

The reason for this, Dove believes, is that "negative energy vibrations you transmit toward them drag down your positive vibes, and you end up lower down on the 'vibes scale' than you want to be. For example, let's say on a scale of one to ten, ten is your highest positive vibration, and one will be your most negative. Even if you have high vibes with most people in your life, just having one person you don't like can drag your vibes down to a lower level."

A couple of suggestions, among others, that Dove has to counteract those negative vibes is to focus on the good. Most people, she says, have some redeeming qualities. "Remember that everyone is born filled with love, joy, and inner peace."

Another one of her suggestions, and one that I was talking about earlier, is that, "We get what we vibrate. If we speak to people in anger, that's what we get back. If we are disrespectful, mean, and insincere, that's what we get back."

While this may sound like New Age pie-in the-sky thinking, research is proving the positive effects of gratitude. In one study, for example, associate professor Francesca Gino, at Harvard Business School, looked at forty-one university fund-raisers. The director of the school visited half of the fund-raisers in person, telling them, "I am very grateful for your hard work. We sincerely appreciate your contributions to the university." The second group received no such expressions of gratitude. Gino found that "the expression of gratitude increased the number of calls [made by the fund-raisers] by more than fifty percent" for the week. Fund-raisers who received no thanks made about the same number of calls as the previous week.

Other studies have shown that expressions of gratitude can help, among other things, with a person's self-worth, with connecting to something larger than themselves, with relationships and with happiness or well-being.

In other words, whether you are seeking more money or greater peace of mind, it pays to say "thanks."

P.S.: And while we are at it, don't forget to say, "You're welcome" too. So many people have replaced a response of "you're welcome" with "no problem" which is negative considering that it implies that there was a problem in the first place, which in most cases there probably wasn't.

~~~~~~~~~~~~~~~~~~~~~~~~~~~~

Gratitude and the Machine

"Rushing to finish some paperwork on a deadline, I ran to the copy/fax machine to send an important document to my colleague at Unity Worldwide. Yes, in our office I still use the fax machine, because for some reason that none of our IT experts can figure out, the scanner function doesn't work with my computer. When I got back to my desk, there was an email from Unity stating that while they had received the fax, it was illegible.

"I sent a reply stating that I had been frustrated all day long about our office equipment and the problems they were causing me. She replied, 'Hummm... I wonder if there is an effective affirmation for frustrating equipment.' She gently reminded me that my first job is to give thanks!

"How often is it that we get caught up in the frustration and fail to see the wonder of all that we have and all that we can do in the first place? While the equipment is not working like I think it should, I spent the morning doing work electronically that just a few short years ago would have been impossible. So my affirmation is: 'I am grateful for the wonders of modern technology.'

"And to put feet to my prayer this morning, I am on my way to purchase a new printer/scanner/copier/fax for the office!"

—Ken Daigle,
Unity San Francisco

Follow-Up

Every morning, before I even put one foot on the floor, I think of one thing for which I am thankful. Starting with a positive thought and reminding myself of the good things I have in life gives me perspective for the day, should any unpleasantness unfold.

—MICHAEL ZWICK,
President, Assets International

There have been a number of studies about the value of being grateful. One, done by psychology professors Robert Emmons and Michael McCullough, found that those who wrote down five reasons to be grateful every day experienced more optimism and had healthier habits than those who recorded struggles.

So stop for a moment right now and write down seven things for which you are grateful. Focus on one of these things each day of this week. It can change your day from a negative one to a positive one.

Or you can do what authors Mark Williams and Danny Penman suggest which they call the "Ten-finger Gratitude Exercise." They recommend that "once a day you should bring to mind ten things that you are grateful for, counting them on your fingers. It is important to get to ten things, even when it becomes increasingly harder after three or four. This is exactly what the exercise is for—intentionally bringing into awareness the tiny, previously unnoticed elements of the day."

Gratitude can also be an important element in maintaining relationships. One study that I found amazing was that of John Gottman from the University of Washington. With ninety percent accuracy, he can predict which marriages might flourish and which might flounder. The key to a happy marriage, he says, is that for every negative expression, such as a complaint, put-down, frown, or an encounter of anger, there needs to be about five positive ones, such as a compliment, a smile, laughter, or appreciation and gratitude.

One simple way to remind yourself to be grateful is to carry a small stone or marble in your pocket. Every time you see or touch it, stop and be thankful for something around you.

I'd also like to share with you about two colleagues of mine, Helen Bzdel and Irene Chaya Doniger, who started what they call The Gratitude Project. They made a pact with each other that they would post three things of gratitude on Facebook every day, no matter how silly or small. They were originally only going to do it for thirty days; as of this writing they are approaching three hundred days and show no signs of stopping.

One of their rules is that no posts can be repeated because, as Doniger points out, "By not repeating, I am forced to look for new things for which I am grateful. It also has helped me develop the habit of finding the good even in difficult times." They post them on Facebook, instead of just writing them in a journal, in order to inspire others to do the same thing. And, "Knowing people are looking for them actually motivates me to keep going."

"Yes," Doniger continues, "there have been days where, on first blush, I thought about skipping the day because there was so much trouble going on. So then I'd ask myself, 'Well, if you wanted to be grateful for something today, what might that be? Anything nice happen today?' Even on the days when my immediate thought is 'No,' I wind up with a smile and come up with something for which I am sincerely grateful."

So, take a tip from Bzdel and Doniger, or from the other suggestions offered here. Instead of focusing on the things that are messing up your day, count your blessings and say "Thank you" for all those wonderful things around you today and every day.

Lighten-Up

I feel a very unusual sensation—if it is not indigestion, I think it must be gratitude.

—BENJAMIN DISRAELI, *British politician*

Leah Dieterich's mother told her to always write thank-you notes, so now she does, to everything and anything. A devoted thank-you note blogger, she writes thank-you notes daily not only to people she admires but also to such inanimate objects such as her heater, cities, and her dead potted orange tree.

So, taking Leah's lead, identify one thing each day this week that annoyed you and write a note of gratitude to it. It could be the clerk who was rude to you at the checkout counter or the one who cheated you when they gave you change. Or, it could be an inanimate object like your microwave that took too long to boil your tea water, a water heater that is not working, a slow elevator, a dead car battery, or the ninety-seven emails that came in within the last ten minutes.

Your note doesn't have to be serious. Leah, for example,

often writes to people and things in a humorous way:

Dear Man Who Punched Out the Back Windshield of a Mini Cooper in Mexico City,

Thanks for acting out your macho road rage five feet in front of us for providing me with enough danger and violence to shake me up and give me a good story to tell, but for not being disturbing enough to give me nightmares. Thanks also for reminding me yet again to never give people the finger while I'm driving.

Take it easy,
Leah

Dear Curse Words + Dirty Words,

Thanks for consistently being fun to say. Few words feel as good coming out of my mouth.

Cheers,
Leah

Note: More of Dieterich's lighthearted letters can be found on her blog page (thxthxthx.com) and in her book, *thxthxthx: Thank Goodness for Everything.*

BE GRATEFUL FOR NOT-SO-GREAT STUFF

⌘

Gratitude is medicine for a heart devastated by tragedy. If you can only be thankful for the blue sky, then do so.

—RICHELLE E. GOODRICH,
author

EARLIER IN THE book, I talked about getting a speeding ticket. Not a happy event. Yet, looking back, I realize that the idea for this book would never have occurred to me without getting that ticket. What I have also realized is that sometimes the negative things in our life are there to help us see things we might not have otherwise seen. And so we need to be grateful for everything in our life, even the not-so-great stuff.

Many of us give thanks for the good things in our life... our job, our friends and family, our home, etc. That is important. But it is perhaps even more important, if we are not to let anything ruin our day, to give thanks for those things that happen to us that are not so wonderful—for our irritations, upsets, losses, and setbacks.

Why? Because those seemingly troublesome things can be our greatest teachers and help us develop our tolerance, compassion, and, perhaps, a greater spirituality.

Yes, I said to give thanks for the annoyances in your life because they can be our greatest teachers and help us grow. I've noticed, and maybe you have too, that we don't grow much spiritually when all is going well. We learn and grow through our trials and tribulations. It is those hard times, those knocks on the head that wake us up and teach us lessons we may not have learned otherwise. Sorry, folks, but that's the way human nature operates.

Somehow, human beings learn more from negative happenings than from the positive. When good things happen, we might be happy for a short while. But when unfortunate things strike, it often stays with us for a long time. They make us look at our life and the meaning that the setback or heartbreak had in it. Sometimes, it changes the course of our entire life.

Think about the times in your life when you experienced the most personal growth, when you learned some of your greatest lessons. Chances are they were not the happiest of occasions. Chances are they were trying times. Chances too

173

are that after a while, once you got past the hurt, past the darkness, you saw parts of your life in a new way. And, perhaps it even made you tougher and more resilient than ever.

In an article I found online at Halfway Point, author Belinda Munoz suggests being grateful "for the things that challenge us, unwanted things we have to confront, things we can't avoid try as we might, and things that at times turn our world upside down." Among others, she suggests giving thanks:

"For challenges that make us doubt ourselves and our abilities, so that we may see what tough material we're made of.

"For problems that sometimes make being alive difficult, so that we may remember that there's always a solution around the corner to make living worth every second.

"For our bodies that fall ill at times, so that we may value and live each hour and each day fully with a gentle reminder of our mortality.

"For the many mistakes we've made and will make, so that we may honor our humility.

"For the kitchen sink that life may throw at us, so that we may feel fully alive as we fumble, bumble, and stumble through trial by fire."

~~~~~~~~~~~~~~~~~~~~~~~~~~~~

Gratitude and Loss

In her blog, *Give Thanks for this Imperfect Life*, author Elaine Mansfield writes about how, after her husband's death, she was a "harsh-word widowed woman." She kept blaming herself for her husband's death. "Maybe I caused Vic's cancer because I cooked too much tofu or didn't use enough turmeric."

Since that kind of thinking led nowhere, she says, "I focused on gratefulness for the many years with the best friend, lover, and sparring partner. Gratitude for our family and friends too. I thanked the heavens that I was loved fully as many never are."

Mansfield goes on mentioning several other things for which she is grateful. She then notes, "When I miss Vic on Thanksgiving Day, remind me to be grateful for the world that remains rather than longing for a world that could have been."

After we experience a loss, we tend to focus on what we no longer have. As a result we focus our energy on the negative, or what is missing in our life, rather than on the positive, or all of those wonderful things we still have. One of my spiritual teachers once told me that when we want what we don't have, we waste what we do have. To translate that into loss-related situations—to want what is no longer in our life is to waste what still remains. We usually don't think about giving thanks when someone dies. Yet gratitude can be one of the most healing tools we have.

Being grateful for what remains after you have experienced a loss can be a powerful way to deal with, and heal, that loss. Turning your attention on how your life was enriched because that person was in it, for example, rather than on the vacuum the loss created, is a powerful and healthy approach to confronting grief.

After my wife died at the age of thirty-four, my thoughts, as often experienced by someone who is grieving, sometimes turned to darker questions like, "Why is this happening to me?" or "How can I go on with my life without her?"

Grief also brought up a feeling of emptiness, depression, and hopelessness. Once I started to be thankful for all that remained in my life—my daughter, my friends, my work, etc.—I got a glimpse of why I could go on living and, in fact, fully enjoy life again.

Gratitude has the power to help those in mourning rise above their loss. It is life affirming. It can provide hope. And, perhaps most important, it can help us let go of the past and focus on the abundance that surrounds us now.

~~~~~~~~~~~~~~~~~~~~~~~~

Follow-Up

Those with a grateful mindset tend to see the message in the mess. And even though life may knock them down, the grateful find reasons, if even small ones, to get up.

—STEVE MARABOLI,
author and speaker

In my book, *Learning to Laugh When You Feel Like Crying*, I suggest a simple way to move toward being grateful after a loss:

Tomorrow morning, before you get out of bed, think of at least one thing that you are thankful for. And then, when you get out of bed, start writing down all the wonderful things in your life, including some of the most simple. You can, for example, be thankful for the neighbor who cried with you; the friends you have; a rainbow; flowers in the park; and a cup of tea.

Those are just a few little gratitudes that can keep you afloat while you are in a sea of grief. But you might also want to note some of the bigger things for which you are grateful. For example, that the deceased was in your life; the lessons you learned from them; and that their spirit still lives within you.

Lighten-Up

A group of seniors were sitting around talking about all of their ailments.

"My cataracts are so bad, I can't even see my coffee," said one lady. "Yes, I know," said another. "I forget where I am or where I'm going."

"And my blood pressure pills make me dizzy!" exclaimed one woman.

"I guess that's the price we pay for getting old," winced an old man as he slowly shook his head.

The others nodded in agreement. "Well, count your blessings," said a woman cheerfully. "Thank God we can all still drive."

BE KIND

⌘

How people treat you is their karma;
how you react is yours.

—WAYNE DYER,
author and speaker

A COUPLE OF years ago, I was hired to do a two-and-a-half-day weekend retreat with burn survivors, their families, and their caregivers. I was brought in to teach them how to lighten up.

It was the first time I had ever worked with people who were severely burned. It was also the longest amount of time I had ever spent with any group in my twenty-plus years of being a professional speaker. On Friday night, I had an introductory session with them. On Saturday, they all participated in an all-day workshop. And finally, on Sunday morning, I did a wrap-up segment with the group. It was the most challenging workshop I had ever done in my speaking career, and perhaps the most gratifying.

When I was first asked to do the retreat, I didn't know how I could possibly teach this group of people to laugh when they had been through such a horrific ordeal. I didn't know how I would react to their disfigurement. I didn't know how I could sustain such a long period of time with them. Would I have enough material to fill the weekend? Would it be relevant to them? After all, they had been through hell. I hadn't.

The truth was that all my fears were unfounded. They loved what I did. They jumped at any chance to laugh. And once I got over the initial shock of seeing their deformities, all I could see was their radiant and beautiful spirits. They didn't know it, but they taught me more than I taught them.

They taught me about courage.

They taught me about unconditional love as I watched their caretakers and loved ones attend to the burn survivor's every need.

They taught me that in spite of what they went through, they could laugh. In fact, they craved it.

One of the processes I did with them was a real eye-opener both for them and for me. I showed them a video of another burn survivor, a professional speaker colleague of mine named W Mitchell. He was not only severely burned in a motorcycle accident but just as he was recovering from that ordeal he also lost the use of his legs when his private plane crashed.

After viewing his video, I asked each person in the group to make a list of all the qualities in Mitchell that they most admired. I then asked them to highlight three of those traits that they also saw in themselves. Each person in the room then shared those assets with the group. There were many tears shed as the burn survivors realized that they, like Mitchell, were courageous, heroic, and brave too.

The reason I'm sharing this story with you is that the qualities that you admire in others are some of the same ones you have within yourself. And this goes for both the qualities you admire and, perhaps even more importantly, those that repel you.

So the next time some negative aspect of someone annoys you, when someone yells at you or makes you angry, when someone says or does something you don't like, remember that you probably have those same traits within you or you would not have noticed it in them. The best you can do in that situation, therefore, is to be kind to them because, on some level, you are just like them.

~~~~~~~~~~~~~~~~~~~~~~~~~~~~~~~

Everyday Survival Kit

These are the items everyone should have in their survival kit:

Toothpick
Rubber band
Band-Aid®
Pencil
Eraser
Chewing gum
Mint
Candy kiss
Tea bag

And here's why:

Toothpick: to remind you to pick out the good qualities in others.

Rubber band: to remind you to be flexible. Things might not always go the way you want, but they will work out.

Band-Aid®: to remind you to heal hurt feelings, yours or someone else's.

Pencil: to remind you to list your blessings every day.

Eraser: to remind you that everyone makes mistakes, and it's O.K.

Chewing gum: to remind you to stick with it and you can accomplish anything.

Mint: to remind you that you are worth a mint to your Heavenly Father.

Candy kiss: to remind you that everyone needs a kiss or a hug every day.

Tea bag: to remind you to relax daily and go over that list of God's blessings.

—Barbara Glanz, *Priceless Gifts*

Follow-Up

Ask yourself: Have you been kind today? Make kind-ness your modus operandi and change your world.

—ANNIE LENNOX,
singer and songwriter

In 2013, author George Saunders delivered the convocation speech at Syracuse University. In part, he talked about regrets and shared with the audience that what he regretted most in his life was "failures of kindness." He told the graduates, "It's a little facile, maybe, and certainly hard to implement, but I'd say, as a goal in life, you could do worse than: Try to be kinder."

This week take that advice and try to be kinder. Every time you encounter someone who upsets you, stop and ask yourself:

"What is it that annoys me about that person?"

"Do I have that quality within me too?"

"If so, how can I be more kind to them, and in doing so, kinder to myself?"

In addition, spiritual teacher John E. Welshons suggests that each day you ask yourself the following questions:

"What can I do today to make this world a better place?"

"Can I forgive the slights?"

"Can I see that everyone is suffering about something?"

"Can I meet harshness and disconnection with love and kindness?"

"What small things can I do to heal my heart, my community, and our planet?"

Lighten-Up

The Hebrew word "mitzvah" has several meanings including "commandment." In contemporary times it also has come to express an act of kindness or doing a good.

When virtuous Fred Danforth died, he was sure he qualified for paradise but was turned down when the admitting angel learned he was totally sinless.

"But I don't understand. I've lived a righteous life!" Fred protested.

"Let me explain," said the angel. "While it's true that paradise is set aside for exemplary people, not one of them is completely without sin, and it just wouldn't be fair to subject them to the discomfort of having someone around who's never transgressed."

"Fair! Do you think *I'm* being treated fairly?" Fred pleaded.

"Tell you what I'm going to do," said the angel. "You go back to earth and commit one sin within twenty-four hours and I'll reconsider your case."

"But I don't know how to sin."

"Try adultery," suggested the angel.

Fred left, and twelve hours later returned with a big, fat, self-satisfied grin.

"Well, what happened?" asked the angel.

Fred was too embarrassed to speak.

"You gotta tell me to get in," said the angel.

"Well," said Fred, "I met this ugly old woman who had been a widow for thirty years—"

"Stop right there," the angel interrupted. "You blew it. Disqualified!"

"But I sinned!" said Fred.

"That was no sin," the angel whispered. "That was a mitzvah."

—Sol Gordon and Harold Brecher,
Life Is Uncertain...Eat Dessert First!

SEE THE LIGHT IN EVERYONE

⌘

Too often we underestimate the power of a touch, a smile, a kind word, a listening ear, an honest accomplishment, or the smallest act of caring, all of which have the potential to turn a life around.

—LEO BUSCAGLIA,
author and speaker

SEVERAL YEARS AGO, I had cataract surgery. The fifteen-minute surgery was miraculous since I had worn glasses since kindergarten and now only need them for reading or computer work. The one negative thing about having the operation, and it is minor, is that sometimes there are shimmering rainbow-like refractions in my left eye when I'm driving at night or in a room with very bright lighting. It used to annoy me, but now I take it as a reminder that each and every one of us is a shimmering beam of light in this world.

We are all one. We are all spiritual beings. We are all connected.

If you believe otherwise, think of the air you are breathing right now. On some level, the air you have just exhaled will, at some point, be the same air someone else will be inhaling. The struggles you are facing, are being faced by others. Your life changes and challenges are similar to others around the world, some to a greater extent than others but still similar. Take for example, child-raising, supporting a family, or dealing with loss.

So the next time you encounter someone who makes you angry and you are tempted to berate him or her, be kind. Think of them instead as being you, or at least part of you, and how you might feel if someone harshly criticizes you or tells you off.

When I went to grade school we were taught to "Do unto others as you would have them do unto you." It has been many moons since I last sat in a classroom. But that lesson is still as valid today as it was then. Today, however, I have expanded it to include *not* doing anything to hurt anyone and also to seeing the light in everyone.

~~~~~~~~~~~~~~~~~~~~~~~~~~~~~

Making Others Feel Better

In her book, *You Are Not the Target*, Laura Archera Huxley says, "At one time or another the more fortunate among us make three startling discoveries. Discovery number one: Each one of us has, in varying degrees, the power to make others feel better or worse. Discovery number two: Making others feel better is much more fun than making them feel worse. Discovery number three: Making *others* feel better generally makes *us* feel better."

As an example, below are three kind and heartwarming things people have done to make others feel better.

After Hurricane Sandy, when most of their neighborhood was without electricity, a couple in New York City hung several power strips on their front gate with a note that read: "We have power. Please feel free to charge your phone!"

Whenever a security guard at Disney's Magic Kingdom sees a young child dressed up in a princess costume, he goes over to them and says, "Excuse me, Princess, can I have your autograph?" The little girls are delighted that the guard thinks that they are real princesses.

Commuters at Earl's Court tube station in London last year received a heartwarming message during the rush hour. The station put this on the whiteboard near the entrance: "You...yes, you. The one reading this. You are beautiful, kind, sweet, amazing, and simply the best at being you. Never forget that."

~~~~~~~~~~~~~~~~~~~~~~~~~~~~

Follow-Up

Do your little bit of good where you are; it's those little bits of good put together that overwhelm the world.

—DESMOND TUTU,
Nobel Peace Prize recipient

The bottom line is that we are all one. The homeless person, who is asking for a handout on the street, could easily be you. Your boss, who is ranting and raving about something that did not go well, could also be you. Just as the person in front of you at the supermarket who is taking forever to unload their grocery cart, count their cash, and bag their groceries, could be you too.

Knowing that, as you go through your day, think about doing something nice for someone else. For example: Compliment someone at work on how especially nice they look. Smile and say hello to a stranger you encounter on the street. Get up and give a seat to someone on the bus. At home, praise your child for something they did or for the meal your spouse just prepared. Hold the door open for someone behind you.

The great thing about taking such actions is that it brings double pleasure, both for the giver and receiver. I've recently experienced that several times.

Knowing that a couple of friends and acquaintances were having difficulty with finances, I sent them each a check. There was no special occasion, nothing to celebrate, just an ordinary day and a chance to make their day. I felt good about it because I had the resources to do so and they were not only surprised but also overjoyed at the unexpected gift. One person noted, "I am bleary-eyed from the tears that flowed freely upon receipt of your generous gift.... I was praying for a miracle when your gift arrived."

Double pleasure. I lifted their spirits and they warmed my heart.

Not only that but by doing something for someone else, I, according to recent studies, bolstered my well-being too. Researchers have shown that there is a direct correlation between giving, good health, and happiness.

In one of the most famous studies about being kind, students were asked to practice five random acts of kindness a week for six weeks. Those who did had a more than forty percent increase in their happiness levels over those who did not.

With such a simple way of taking back your power when someone is seemingly ruining your day, what are you waiting for? You can increase your happiness levels now.

Just ask yourself: "What can I do for someone else today?"

Lighten-Up

A travel agent looked up from his desk to see an older lady and an older gentleman peering in the shop window at the posters showing the glamorous destinations around the world. The agent had had a good week and the dejected couple gave him a rare feeling of generosity.

He called them into his shop and said, "I know that on your pension you could never hope to have a holiday, so I am sending you off to a fabulous resort at my expense, and I won't take no for an answer."

He took them inside and asked his secretary to write two flight tickets and book a room in a five-star hotel. They, as can be expected, gladly accepted, and were on their way.

About a month later the little lady came in to his shop. "And how did you like your holiday?" he asked eagerly.

"The flight was exciting and the room was lovely," she answered. "I've come to thank you. But, one thing puzzled me. Who was that old guy I had to share the room with?"

BECOME A CAMERA

⌘

As a photographer, I have a choice of what lens I put on my camera; a choice of how I am going to view the world. I choose to celebrate. Why? Because it imbues me with gratitude, because it allows me to see the best in people and situations, because it fills me with energy.

—DEWITT JONES,
photojournalist

WHEN I WAS a hospice volunteer, I visited an elderly woman who would usually be lying on the couch watching some TV game show when I arrived. The sound would be blaring away making conversation impossible. Finally, frustrated, I shouted over the high volume, "Is there anything

I can do for you?" She responded, "Do you know how to dance?" Being one of my first clients, I was anxious to help her. So I got up and danced around the room.

Then I sat down and asked her if she enjoyed it. She simply shrugged her shoulders. Feeling even more frustrated, I shouted even louder, "I'm a hospice volunteer. I'm here to help you. Is there anything I can do for you?" There was a long silence and then she asked, "Do you know how to disco?" And I, being a hospice volunteer that would do anything for a patient, got up and discoed around the room to the music of *Dating Game*.

Again, I sat down and asked her if there was anything else I could do. After a long silence, she said, "You could leave!"

My heart sank and I felt as if I had failed the patient. I didn't tell the family what happened when they returned. But I did tell the staff when I got back to the hospice office. And as soon as they heard my story, they all burst out in laughter. I didn't see the humor in it until they made me realize, that if there had been a camera on the ceiling in the corner of the room filming my disco dancing for a dying lady to the music of *Dating Game*, how funny that might be. And they were right. When I got that image in my head, I started to laugh too.

That dying patient taught me a couple of great lessons for which I am grateful. First, as a caregiver, you don't call the shots, the patient does. If they want to cry, you can cry with them. If they want to laugh, then you can laugh with them. It is their agenda, not yours.

But the bigger lesson here is that other people have their agendas and you don't have to get caught up in them. You have the power to become a camera and merely observe what is happening instead of reacting to it.

~~~~~~~~~~~~~~~~~~~~~~~~~~~~~~~

Zoom Out

The dying lady mentioned above taught me another great life lesson. Most of us have blinders on and can only see our own tiny part of the world. We get so shortsighted in our circumstances that we cannot see the bigger picture.

Blinders might serve a horse well, particularly if you are riding it and don't want it to be distracted on the path on which you are headed.

Blinders might be useful for us too, especially when we need to get a task done and don't want to be interrupted. But more often than not, we have a narrow view, or "zoomed-in" perspective of the world, especially when someone is baiting our anger or lashing out at us. Getting caught up in all of that doesn't serve us because it gives us only a limited picture of the situation.

What would serve us better, would be to "zoom out," to set our camera on a wide-angle lens, in order to see the bigger picture and not get so caught up in a situation. Zooming out would help us step back, disengage, and see what is happening from a more encompassing vantage point.

In his book, *The Four Agreements Companion Book*, author don Miguel Ruiz says that "When we attach to an object, to our beliefs, to a person we love, it is just as if we are stuck in the zoom-in mode, and all we see is the smallest part of Life." But when we zoom out, he says, "All your troubles are a tiny speck on the face of the earth."

Zooming out and disengaging from the things that annoy you would help you see that perhaps you are not always right and even if you are, it might be a greater good to not get caught up in a situation and simply move on. It would help you have a more contented, less confrontational experience.

When you "zoom out" of an upsetting situation, you get to see more possibilities. As a result, your anger, upset, or frustration has at least the potential of being abated. You may not see that at the moment. That's because what you are dealing with might seem too huge in your picture for you to see anything else. But if you are willing to take your blinders off and use a wide-angle lens, you might see a plethora of possibilities available to you other than being upset.

Follow-Up

*Look and think before opening the shutter. The heart
and mind are the true lens of the camera.*

—YOUSUF KARSH,
photographer

If there is only one thing you do today to help you have a happier, healthier week, remember that there is always an imaginary camera filming your reactions to situations. It can zoom in and see you angry and upset or it can zoom out and see you as the happy person you were meant to be.

How do you want to be seen when it is filmed and posted on Facebook or YouTube?

Lighten-Up

Top five reasons to date a photographer: They make things develop. They work well on many settings. They know how to focus. They can make big things look small and small things look big. They zoom in and out. And in and out and in and out and in and out...

FORGET WHAT YOU KNOW

⌘

I have approximate answers and possible beliefs and different degrees of certainty about different things, but I'm not absolutely sure about anything.

—RICHARD FEYNMAN,
physicist and Nobel Prize recipient

I HAVE A friend who frequently speaks with great authority and often insists that he is right, even when he is not. I have confronted him about this on several occasions but it is a losing battle. He either continues to insist he is right, even when I have proof otherwise, or he brushes over the facts. I have given up pointing out his errors because it only ruins my day. So I let him carry on, and I move on.

How often are your days ruined because you get into a

confrontation insisting you are right? Even if you're right, you are making the other person wrong. And if you maintain your self-righteous stance, you shut the door and leave no room for anything else or any meeting in the middle.

But you know what? You don't have to be right all the time. You don't have to have all the answers—and you probably never will. The truth is that the highest form of knowing is actually "not knowing" because it leaves the door open to all kinds of possibilities and discoveries.

In his book, *Fire in the Belly*, author Sam Keen writes, "A mountain man was once asked if he often got lost. 'No,' he replied. 'I've never been lost. But sometimes for a month or two, I didn't know how to get to where I was going.'"

It is important to be clear in which direction you want to go. But sometimes, not knowing can lead to amazing places. Christopher Columbus, for example, set sail thinking he was going to discover a shorter route to India. What he discovered was a whole new world.

"Explorers need to know how to get lost comfortably," says Keen. "The adventure of the spirit begins when we stop pretending and performing and accept our confusion and insecurity." To that "confusion" and "insecurity" we might also want to add the Zen Buddhism concept of "beginner's mind." It refers to being open and eager without a preconception of the way things should be. This concept is useful for having a day that is not ruined by anyone or any situation because it helps us see things, like a child, without fixed ideas of the way we think things should be.

Mary Jaksch, a psychotherapist and Zen Master who lives in New Zealand, asks a very good question about beginner's mind—"What if we had that approach to everything we did? What would life be like?"

For one thing, Jaksch says, that "in martial arts, a *don't know* mind is the wisdom of the warrior. Because we can easily get it wrong by prejudging a situation.... A don't know mind leaves room for intuition." Her advice: "Let go of knowing—that's real wisdom."

A second thing Jaksch suggests is that we let go of being an expert. "If I let go of being an expert, I can listen to others with an open mind. Then I can find that even a beginner has something to teach me."

In this confusing and seemingly harsh world, you may be at a loss for answers to difficult questions or challenging situations. Perhaps that is O.K. Answers may come later. For now, you may just want to hang out with a beginner's mind and remember what Zen master Shunryu Suzuki said, "If your mind is empty, it is always ready for anything, it is open to everything. In the beginner's mind there are many possibilities, but in the expert's mind there are few."

Last year, due to the cancellation of two of the last flights of the evening that I was scheduled to be on, I had to spend the night at the airport. While that may sound awful, it was much better than I expected, mostly because I began to see the situation with beginner's eyes. Since I had never had to do this, in spite of my more than twenty years of heavy travel, it was all new to me—and very exciting.

I never realized how much activity happens at an airport in the middle of the night—workers washing windows, shops getting deliveries, floors being mopped, planes being serviced and lightbulbs being changed. And, yes, there was even some humor as I watched the bizarre scene of other delayed passengers parading around the airport wrapped in blankets or dressed in their patterned pajamas, flannel bathrobes, and pink fluffy slippers.

Follow-Up

*When you fully accept that you don't know, you actu-
ally enter a state of peace and clarity that is closer
to who you truly are than thought could ever be.
Defining yourself through thought is limiting yourself.*

—ECKHART TOLLE,
A New Earth

Years ago, when personal growth seminars were popular, I took one with Ken Keyes, Jr., a spiritual teacher and author. Looking back, I realize now that one of the processes we did involved experiencing an object with a beginner's mind.

First we held a single raisin in our hand. We spent a long time looking at it—the shape, the texture, and the color. After close examination, we each realized that our raisin was different from anyone else's in the entire group. Our little dried grape was special. No other raisin in the world was exactly the same as the one we were holding.

Then we put the raisin in our mouth and took an equally long time feeling the texture, investigating the surface with our tongue, and finally biting down on it. After that we very slowly chewed it. Again noticing the texture, the roughness of the outside, and the sweetness of the inside.

This process was a most intense experience for me—a simple exercise that I have remembered for many years. It taught me a great lesson. How often do I eat without really looking carefully at, or truly tasting, what I am eating?

It also taught me to take time to look at things with a beginner's mind and, although I have to remind myself over and over about this, to fully appreciate the special little things in everyday life.

Since beginner's mind can help you see things in a new way, rather than automatically responding with the same old patterns of behavior, try this exercise with someone who has upset you this week:

1. Find a comfortable place to sit. Take a few deep breaths and set your intentions to see things with a beginner's mind.

2. If you have a photo of the person who has distressed you this week, take it out and look at it for several minutes. If you do not have a photo, then imagine the face of that person in your mind.

3. Now imagine that you are from another planet and have never seen anything like them before. Take some time to really look at that person without judging them.

4. Notice that person's unique qualities. Note the things you really like about the way they look or find especially appealing about them. Become aware of some of their inner qualities that you admire that perhaps you've never seen before.

5. After about five minutes, reflect on this exercise. Did you learn anything new about this person? Did seeing the person from a beginner's mind change your anger or being upset with them? Might you react differently to this person the next time you encounter them?

Lighten-Up

You must unlearn what you have learned.

—YODA,
Star Wars *fictional character*

It was an extremely busy Friday night at the Denver airport. Many business travelers were trying to get home. Suddenly there was an announcement at the gate. "Due to an approaching lightning storm, most of the flights tonight have been cancelled."

A well-dressed man pushed his way to the head of the line and blared at the gate agent, "I don't care what you have to do, you must get me out of here tonight."

Keeping her calm in the midst of this barrage, the agent said, "I'm sorry, sir, but I'm doing the best I can."

Not taking that for an answer, the passenger raised his voice even louder and declared, "You've got to get me on a plane tonight. Do you know who I am? Do you know who I am?"

The gate agent reached for the microphone and broadcast, "There is a man at the counter who doesn't know who he is. Can someone please come and claim him?"

SEE THINGS
AS THEY REALLY ARE

⌘

Many of our thoughts, fears, and worries are like junk
mail. We don't need to open them and explore them.
No need to save them. No need to pay a lot of atten-
tion to them and take them so seriously. Don't believe
everything you think.

—ALAN GETTIS,
psychologist

ONE DAY I was giving a public presentation at a Florida
hospital. The audience was very receptive and seemed to
really enjoy the talk. One woman, who was seated in the
front row, was particularly engaged in what I was saying.
Throughout the program, she nodded her head in agreement with my main points. But then, when the presentation

was over, I noticed that her head kept bobbing up and down long after I finished speaking.

That day I learned that things are not always as they seem.

Years ago, one of my favorite television programs was Rod Serling's *The Twilight Zone.* I still recall one of the episodes in which two teenage girls are riding on the subway. To amuse themselves, they are playing a game in which they try and guess what the people sitting opposite them do. They giggle as they whisper what they are thinking to each other. Then one of them says that the man opposite them is a murderer. The man overhears them and follows them for the rest of the program.

I don't recall how the show ended but it illustrates an important point about how we often put a label on someone else without even knowing that person. Just as the teenagers didn't really know anything about the man they thought was a murderer.

So too, we frequently don't know why people react the way they do. We make assumptions that can stress us out and ruin our day. We often operate with a preconceived notion of how things should be instead of the way they are. Many times, in fact, we gather evidence and build a case to make ourselves right and someone else wrong. We forget, as illustrated in the following story from the Jewish tradition, that there is often more than one side to every story:

Two men come to the rabbi's study to settle a dispute. The rabbi's wife is also seated in the room.

The first man explains his complaint to the rabbi: the story is such and so, and he has to do this and he has to do that. He gives a fine account and argues his case clearly.

The rabbi declares, "You're right."

Then the other man presents his side. He speaks with such passion and persuasion that the rabbi says to him, "You're right, too."

After they leave, the rabbi's wife is distraught and says to her husband, "They have conflicting stories. How can you say that both of them are right? When one wins, the other must lose."

The rabbi thinks long and hard and finally says to his wife, "You know, dear, you're right."

And from the Sufi tradition comes another teaching story illustrating that we can prove anything but it doesn't always make it right:

Nasrudin was throwing handfuls of crumbs around the house.

"What are you doing?" someone asked him.

"Keeping the tigers away."

"But there are no tigers in these parts."

"That's right. Effective, isn't it?"

~~~~~~~~~~~~~~~~~~~~~~~~~~~~~

Who Moved My Cookie?

"I was a bit early for the train...[so] I went to get myself a newspaper to do the crossword, and a cup of coffee and a packet of cookies. I went and sat at a table.... There's a guy sitting opposite me, perfectly ordinary-looking guy wearing a business suit, carrying a briefcase. It didn't look like he was going to do anything weird. What he did was this: He suddenly leaned across, picked up the packet of cookies, tore it open, took one out, and ate it.

"Now this, I have to say, is the sort of thing the British are bad at dealing with.... But in the end, I did what any red-blooded Englishman would do: I ignored it. And I stared at the newspaper, took a sip of coffee, tried to do a clue in the newspaper, couldn't do anything and thought, *What am I going to do...?*

"I tried very hard not to notice the fact that the packet was already mysteriously opened. I took out a cookie for myself. I thought, *That settled him.* But it hadn't because a moment or two later he did it again. He took another cookie....

"We went through the whole packet like this.... He took one, I took one, he took one, I took one. Finally, when we got to the end, he stood up and walked away. Well, we exchanged meaningful looks, then he walked away, and I breathed a sigh of relief and sat back.

"A moment or two later the train was coming in, so I tossed back the rest of my coffee, stood up, picked up the newspaper and underneath the newspaper were my cookies. The thing I like particularly about this story is the sensation that somewhere in England there has been wandering around for the last quarter-century a perfectly ordinary guy who's had the same exact story; only he doesn't have the punch line."

—Douglas Adams,
English writer

Follow-Up

What concerns me is not the way things are, but rather the way people think things are.

—EPICTETUS,
Greek philosopher

A television show I used to like when I was younger was *What's My Line?* It featured a panel of four celebrities who tried to guess, similar to the story above about the girls on the subway, what was the guest's occupation.

With a slight twist, this might be a good game to play when someone is ruining your day. Instead of asking the annoying "guest" in your life, "What's your line?", in your mind ask them, "What's your problem?"

In other words, instead of trying to be right or to win an argument, turn things around by throwing the ball back in their court. You may not know why the other person is acting the way they are, but you can control how you react and not let their actions ruin your day.

I remember how my young nephew, who is deaf, would react when people did not understand what he was saying. He would completely turn things around and ask them, "What's wrong with you?"

Lighten-Up

His request approved, a photographer from a major news service called the local airport to charter a flight. He was told a twin-engine plane would be waiting for him when he got there.

Arriving at the airfield, he spotted a plane warming up outside a hangar. He jumped in with his bag, slammed the door shut, and shouted, "Let's go."

The pilot taxied out, swung the plane into the wind and took off.

Once in the air, the photographer instructed the pilot, "Fly over the valley, and make low passes, so I can take pictures of the fires on the hillsides."

"Why?" asked the pilot.

"Because I'm a newspaper photographer," he responded, "and I need to get some close-up shots."

The pilot was strangely silent for a moment, finally he stammered, "So, what you're telling me, is...you're *not* my flight instructor?"

SEEK SILENCE

⌘

*In the attitude of silence, the soul finds the path in
a clearer light, and what is elusive and deceptive
resolves itself into crystal clearness.*

—MAHATMA GANDHI,
spiritual leader

TODAY, WE PROCESS more information in twenty-four
hours than our ancestors did in one year. The Internet
provides more information than we could ever use in multiple
lifetimes. Texting keeps us constantly connected. Emails
continually bombard us. Twitter brings us instant messages
from around the world. Facebook friends alert us to what
they are doing on a minute-to-minute basis. Hundreds of
television channels give us more choices than ever before.

Is it no wonder that we are overloaded and over-whelmed?

Is it no wonder that we don't have time to do all that we want to do?

Is it no wonder that we are stressed out?

One of the things that can help you deal with all of these technical demands is to take time to disconnect, to be silent. It seems paradoxical to add one more thing to your plate that is already filled to capacity. But the act of being silent can actually help you become more focused and less stressed. Sometimes our inner self knows exactly what to do. But to access the answer, we need to get quiet to hear it. We need to stop our mind chatter and listen.

"Silence creates the space for you to think and thus see reality more clearly," says Mark Divine, a retired commander of the U.S. Navy SEALs. "With practice," he says, "we can gain complete control over the critical mind (the one that incorrectly inflates or deflates us) and tap into our fuller mental powers. In addition to better seeing ourselves, we also better see reality with a clear, still mind, so we make improved decisions and gain more insight."

Buddhist teacher Kadam Morten illustrated this point by using a major workplace stress producer for many people—their boss. Workers often feel that the boss is pressuring them. "But if that was the case," says Morten, "everyone would be tense when they encountered the boss. So, this is obviously how *you* are perceiving your boss. You have created the stress-inducing boss."

This is wonderful to hear, Morten notes. "Since you are the creator of the stress-inducing boss, then you can actually do something about it." In other words, your boss is like a mirror, reflecting back at you "your own uncontrolled states of mind." To control those thoughts, Morten suggests meditation to nurture stillness to see what comes up in your mind about the boss.

In the silence of meditation, says Morten, you might see what would be the better response for your being upset with the boss and blaming your stress on him or her. For example, "My boss is helping me train my mind." Or, "My boss is helping me develop patience." In other words, through silence, says Morten, the "boss is transformed from someone who is an obstacle in your life to actually someone who is helping you to develop good."

To find more silence in a noisy world is not easy. But it is possible. You can turn down the volume to tune up your life. Below are just three ideas to consider:

Control the phone. At dinnertime, when those pesky solicitors tend to call, you can choose not answer it. Or, if you do answer the phone, immediately say something like, "Can I call you back later?" If it's a friend they usually say, "Yes." If it's a salesperson they usually hang up.

My mother-in-law had a great comeback after a salesman phoned asking to speak to her recently deceased husband. When she said that he wasn't home, the salesperson wanted to know where he could find him. My mother-in-law replied, "If you want to speak to my husband, you'll have to go to Hell."

Play in the dirt. Gardens are a wonderful way to enjoy silence and just be with nature as long as you don't carry your cell phone with you when you are tending them. And even if you live in an apartment you can have a small planter, window box, a variety of houseplants, or maybe even a roof garden.

Walk your dog. If you have a dog, taking them out for a walk is not only a wonderful way to get some exercise but also to get some silence, provided you leave your phone at home. And an extra bonus is that silence could also be a great way to stimulate your creativity.

When I was writing one of my books, *The Courage to Laugh*, sometimes the words weren't flowing. So I'd stop and take my dog for a walk. More often than not, the ideas I was struggling with resolved themselves during the walk. In fact, part of the dedication in that book, went to thanking my dog. It reads: "Perhaps the person who unknowingly contributed most to this book is not a person at all. It is my dog, Josh. I have learned a lot from Josh, including unconditional love, staying in the present, and going with the flow. But most of all, I acknowledge Josh as a major contributor because it was on our morning walks together that I first got, and then clarified, many ideas in this book. Thanks, Josh!"

And if you don't have a dog you could volunteer to walk someone else's.

Language Is Tasting

A Zen master was resting with his disciple. At one point, he took a melon out of his bag and cut it in half for them to eat.

In the middle of the meal, the disciple said, "My wise teacher, I know that everything you do has a meaning. Sharing this melon with me may be a sign that you have something to teach me."

The master continued eating in silence.

"I understand the hidden question in your silence," insisted the student. "I think it is this: the wonderful taste of this melon that I am experiencing, is it on the melon or on my tongue?"

The master still said nothing.

The student continued, "...And like everything in life, this also has a meaning, I think I'm closer to the answer; the pleasure of the taste is an act of love and interdependence between the two, because without the melon there wouldn't be an object of pleasure, and without the tongue..."

"Enough!" said the master. "The biggest fools are those who consider themselves the most intelligent, and seek an interpretation for everything! The melon is good; please let this be enough. Let me eat it in peace!"

—Paulo Coelho,
Brazilian novelist

Follow-Up

You ask me how I can remain calm and not become upset when those around me are all bustling about. What can I say to you? I did not come into the world to agitate it. Is it not sufficiently agitated already?

—ST. FRANCIS DE SALES,
religious moralist

This week, take time each day and stop for one moment...and listen. You will hear silence speaking. It will be telling you how to focus, be less defensive and more centered.

In *You Can Be Happy No Matter What,* author Richard Carlson reminds us that "new answers don't come from what you already know in the computer part of your brain. They come from...the unknown, quieter part of yourself."

He illustrates this with the familiar story of someone who has lost his or her keys. No matter how much they search where they might be, they can't find them. Then, just when they have given up, the answer to where the keys are pops into his or her head. "You can learn to access and trust...the quiet part of your mind...the wise part of you that knows the answers," says Carlson.

One of the processes Carlson suggests for accessing the quieter, perhaps more knowing parts of our being, he calls our "back-burner." "Each of us has access to a 'back-burner,' a quiet place in the back of the mind where answers and solutions can grow and develop—without the interference of excess thought."

While Carlson suggests that you use this process when you need an answer within a certain time period, I think you can use this process to quiet your mind and quell your anger or upset anytime.

Lighten-Up

Meditate playfully; don't meditate seriously. When you go into the meditation hall, leave your serious faces where you leave your shoes. Let meditation be fun. "Fun" is a very religious word; "seriousness" is very irreligious. If you want to attain to the original mind, you will have to live a very non-serious, though sincere life; you will have to transform your work into play...

—OSHO
Yoga: The Supreme Science, Talk #3

Four monks were meditating in a monastery. All of a sudden the prayer flag on the roof started flapping.

The younger monk came out of his meditation and said: "Flag is flapping."

A more experienced monk said: "Wind is flapping."

A third monk who had been there for more than twenty years said: "Mind is flapping."

The fourth monk who was the eldest said: "Mouths are flapping!"

TAKE A BREATHING BREAK

⌘

If you want to conquer the anxiety of life,
live in the moment, live in the breath.

—AMIT RAY,
author and spiritual teacher

IN *THE OBSERVATION Deck*, a book about writing and writers that was mentioned earlier, author Naomi Epel mentions how the famous mystery writer Sue Grafton uses conscious breathing to start her day. Not only does the exercise help Grafton focus on being more productive, energetic, and imaginative, but it also helps her solve whatever problem she is currently facing in her writing.

Focused breathing can help you deal with any problem you are facing too. One of the most helpful things you can do in stressful, you're-ruining-my-day situations is to stop and remember to breathe.

Of course, we breathe all the time. If we didn't we would be dead. It is our connection to life. It is also our connection to living with less stress.

Breathing happens naturally, so why should we have to remember to breathe? Because when we are stressed, angry, or upset, our breath becomes short and quick. Sometimes we hold our breath. When we tense up, we forget to breathe naturally. As a result, we don't think clearly and our thoughts and actions often escalate.

Stopping and taking a few long deep breaths calms us down, relieves our anxiety, brings us back into the present moment, and helps us focus when things start to spin out of control.

Jon Carlson, a professor of psychology and counseling, says, "The quickest way to clear anxiety out of your body is to take a few deep belly breaths. Chest breathing seems to be wired into anxiety production, while belly breathing is connected to anxiety reduction. If you are anxious, you can wait until you are not anxious and your breathing will slow down. But if you are in a hurry to clear out the anxiety, you can slow down your breath consciously and watch the anxiety go away."

So the quickest way to relieve tension, whether dealing with traffic jams on the highway or confronting someone who irritates you on the road of life, is to stop and take some slow deep breaths.

~~~~~~~~~~~~~~~~~~~~~~~~~~~

Moments

"If I had my life to live over, I'd dare to make more mistakes next time. I'd relax, I would limber up. I would be sillier than I have been this trip. I would take fewer things seriously. I would take more chances. I would climb more mountains and swim more rivers. I would eat more ice cream and less beans. I would perhaps have more actual troubles, but I'd have fewer imaginary ones.

"You see, I'm one of those people who lived sensibly and sanely, hour after hour, day after day. Oh, I've had my moments, and if I had to do it over again, I'd have more of them. In fact, I'd try to have nothing else. Just moments, one after another, instead of living so many years ahead of each day. I've been one of those persons who never goes anywhere without a thermometer, a hot water bottle, a raincoat, and a parachute. If I had to do it again, I would travel lighter than I have.

"If I had my life to live over, I would start barefoot earlier in the spring and stay that way later in the fall. I would go to more dances. I would ride more merry-go-rounds. I would pick more daisies."

—Nadine Stair,
"I'd Pick More Daisies"

~~~~~~~~~~~~~~~~~~~~~~~~~~~

Follow-Up

I've got to keep breathing.
It'll be my worst business mistake if I don't.

—STEVE MARTIN,
comedian

When someone or something is getting your goat, grant yourself just one minute to step back and take a couple of deep conscious breaths. Stop for sixty seconds and concentrate on breathing in and breathing out. Inhale to a count of five, hold for a count of twenty, and then exhale for a count of ten. Do this for just one minute but continue, if needed, for as long as you need to calm down.

Lighten-Up

A couple of hunters are out in the woods when one of them falls to the ground. He doesn't seem to be breathing; his eyes are rolled back in his head. The other guy whips out his cell phone and calls 911. He gasps to the operator, "My friend isn't breathing. I think he is dead. What can I do?"

The operator says, "Just take it easy. First, let's make sure he's dead."

There is silence, and then a shot is heard.

The guy's voice comes back on the line. He says, "O.K., now what?"

CHILL OUT

⌘

*Throw out an alarming alarm clock. If the ring is loud
and strident, you're waking up to instant stress. You
shouldn't be bullied out of bed, just reminded that it's
time to start your day.*

—SHARON GOLD
(attributed)

WHENEVER A COLLEAGUE of mine, Chip Lutz, is stressed
out, he reminds himself of a word that his children often use.
The word is "ch'lax," which is a combination of the words
"chill" and "relax."

In one of his blog postings, Lutz, who is also a professional speaker, as I am, shares about a particularly difficult
day of travel he had getting to a speaking engagement. After

finally reaching his destination at 1:00 A.M., he says, "As I lay there in bed with my mind racing, I knew I had a choice to make. I could choose to stay in a whirlwind of craziness and let my emotions get the best of me or I could choose something else. I chose to focus on coffee. That's all I wanted the next day—a decent cup of coffee. It didn't even have to be great—just decent."

"We all have days that go awry," says Lutz. "Changing our attitude can make it all go a bit smoother." He suggests three ways to do that:

First, change your focus. "Looking forward to that cup of coffee helped me ch'lax."

Second, find some humor. "Yes, the day was frustrating at times, but there were some pretty great moments.... Most of those moments came from thinking about the people I had met during that day."

Third, be grateful. "For example: Even though the day was long, I had my carry-on luggage (with toothbrush), a phone, music, and I was able to find a place to sleep for a few hours...."

Lutz continues, "The next morning I got up early and headed toward the airport... If anything were wrong, I would not have noticed. Everything changed because I changed. That's how life works, isn't it? All of life is made up of moments—good moments and, to put it mildly, not-so-good moments. But, it is also made up of moments of choice—where we can choose how we are going to deal with the things that can batter us around. I chose coffee and it helped me change my perspective, ch'lax, and be thankful for the things that were going right."

All of us have different ways we ch'lax. Like Lutz, you can decide to have a cup of coffee or listen to your favorite music. You can also make a little more effort and get a massage or go see a movie. It doesn't really matter what it is. What is important is to know what helps you "ch'lax" and then do it when things start to get overwhelming.

~~~~~~~~~~~~~~~~~~~~~~~~~~~

One, Two, Three

One-minute meditation:

"1. Create a place of solitude. 2. Sit down. 3. Place your legs in a relaxed but fixed position. 4. Sit up. 5. Set your alarm for exactly one minute. 6. Place your hands in a relaxed but fixed position. 7. Close your eyes. 8. Allow your mind to settle into your breathing. 9. When the alarm sounds, stop."

—Martin Boroson, *One-moment meditation: Stillness for People on the Go*

Two-minute reading:

"Fundamental richness is available in each moment. The key is to relax: relax to a cloud in the sky, relax to a tiny bird with gray wings, relax to the sound of the telephone ringing. We can see the simplicity in things as they are. We can smell things, taste things, feel emotions, and have memories. When we are able to be there without saying, 'I certainly agree with this,' or 'I definitely don't agree with that,' but just be here very directly, then we find fundamental richness everywhere. It is not ours or theirs but is available always to everyone. In raindrops, in blood drops, in heartache, and delight, this wealth is the nature of everything. It is like the sun in that it shines on everyone without discrimination."

—Pema Chödrön,
The Pocket Pema Chödrön

Three-minute garden walk:

Sorry, you will have to find your own garden or perhaps, if none is near, go online to find a virtual one. A favorite of mine is the Japanese Tea Garden in San Francisco (japaneseteagardensf.com).

Follow-Up

The time to relax is when you don't have time for it.

—SYDNEY J. HARRIS,
journalist

What are the things that help you chill out, things that help you relax? And I'm not talking about getting drunk.

I'm talking about getting drunk on life. Make a short list of those things and try doing one of those each day this week. Yes, I know you don't have time to do it but it doesn't take much time. See the above sidebar for a one-minute meditation, a two-minute reading from an inspirational book, or a three-minute walk in a garden. Any of these might be all it takes to help you ch'lax and have a great stress-free day.

Lighten-Up

After my brother and I moved out of the house, our mom got a job at a major kitchen appliance company. As a customer service representative, she got a call from a woman who claimed to be a prominent socialite. The woman complained that she was having an important dinner party that night and her dishwasher, with all her dirty dishes in it, was not working. The woman insisted that a repairman be sent out immediately. My mom told the irate customer that it was impossible; the repairman would be there first thing in the morning. The irate woman shouted, "And what am I supposed to do? I have twelve people coming for dinner tonight and I don't have a clean plate in the house."

My mom calmly replied: "Chill out lady. Just use paper plates."

That was my mom's first and last day on that job.

STOP COMPLAINING

⌘

If you took one-tenth the energy you put into complaining and applied it to solving the problem, you'd be surprised by how well things can work out.... Complaining does not work as a strategy. We all have finite time and energy. Any time we spend whining is unlikely to help us achieve our goals. And it won't make us happier.

—RANDY PAUSCH,
professor

ONCE THERE WAS a very strict Zen monastery. The monks in training who lived there were allowed to say only two words every ten years. One day, the head monk asked a "new" monk for his two words. "Bed hard," the novice replied.

Ten years later the monk was asked again for two words. "Food stinks," he said.

After ten more years, he once again was allowed two words. "I quit!" said the monk.

"Well, I can see why," replied the head monk. "All you ever do is complain."

Complaining doesn't accomplish anything. You either do something to correct the thing you are complaining about or leave it alone and stop complaining. Keep complaining and pretty soon you will be the only one who hears your complaints. "People won't have time for you if you are always angry or complaining," says physicist Stephen Hawking.

On the other hand, researchers are also finding that "effective complaining" might have some mental health benefits. For instance, you may feel satisfied when you complain about an issue and it is resolved by a customer service agent. But, for the most part, ineffective complaining could be detrimental to your health. And that is what we do ninety-nine percent of the time.

For a moment, think about all the things you complain about every day. The weather, the traffic, your boss, your kids, your spouse, the crappy waiter, the less-than-par restaurant meal, the long bank line, the poor store service, the phone-hold, the slowness of the computer, the high prices, the rude people, and on and on.

Complaining about one or two of these a day might not be so bad but researchers are now telling us that we have so many complaints these days that the accumulation of frustration and helplessness can add up and impact our mood, our self-esteem, and, yes, our mental health too.

In an earlier section of the book, I asked if getting angry, upset, or mad serves us. The same could be asked about complaining. And the answer, except perhaps for an occasional complaint, as noted above, would be the same. Complaining doesn't serve us either. It doesn't help us get rid of what irritates us and it doesn't help foster what feeds us. On top of that it can alienate other people around us. And no one has ever achieved health and happiness by complaining.

~~~~~~~~~~~~~~~~~~~~~~~

Kvetching

In Yiddish there is a great word that means to complain and to whine...a lot. That word is "kvetch." While I don't like the negative connotation of constantly complaining, a good kvetch once in a while can accomplish some constructive things.

Kvetching, for example, can relieve stress. Providing your venting doesn't cause stress for others, it can help you get something off your chest even if no one else but you hears it. In addition, it can also be a social icebreaker that bonds you and someone else together as you both kvetch about something that is a common annoyance.

And at times, kvetching can even provide a good

laugh. For example, Roberta's mother bought her first telephone answering machine. Below is what she recorded on it:

"If you want me to make smoked salmon when you come to visit, press 1."

"If you want chopped liver, press 2."

"If you want chicken soup, press 3."

"If you want chicken soup with matzo balls, press 4."

"If you want to know how am I feeling, you must have dialed the wrong number because nobody ever asks me how I am. Who knows, I could even be dead by now."

While I'm not an advocate of complaining, if you can become a Jewish mother and exaggerate your *tsuris* (another Yiddish word loosely meaning aggravation), a limited amount of kvetching for a short while might help you turn a not-so-great day around.

~~~~~~~~~~~~~~~~~~~~~~~~~~~~

Follow-Up

Jews don't sing and pray. They complain. And eat.

—TOM LEVITT,
character in the TV series Smash

In their book, *Work Like Your Dog*, Matt Weinstein and Luke Barber suggest an experiment related to complaining. "Ask your friends if they like being around people who complain a lot. Then ask them if they would prefer someone who doesn't complain much but who occasionally breaks into song. Look critically at people who are chronic complainers and compare your perception of their lives with those who are chronic singers. My guess is that your research will confirm my own findings. Singing has few costs and great benefits, whereas complaining has few benefits and enormous costs."

Complaining seems to be a built-in habit for many people, including myself—I am Jewish after all. Therefore, I'm grateful to Will Bowen, who founded an organization named A Complaint Free World. Their vision is to "see a day when people focus on and speak about what they desire things to be rather than complaining about how things are."

To accomplish that goal, they provide Complaint Free purple bracelets to inspire people to "leave the toxic communication of complaining behind and experience an internal shift toward being more positive, hopeful, and optimistic."

To date, nearly ten million purple Complaint Free bracelets have been sent to people in more than a hundred countries.

You might want to obtain one of their bracelets (acomplaintfreeworld.org) and become a Complaint Free person by wearing one for twenty-one days. The idea is, when you catch yourself complaining, you move the bracelet to the other arm and begin your countdown again. They advise that you stay with the process. "It may take many months but when you reach twenty-one days you will find that your entire life is happier, more loving, and more enjoyable."

Doing the process myself helped me also clarify what a complaint was. It was not just somebody criticizing or grumbling about something or someone. It was also about somebody criticizing or grumbling about something or someone and *not* doing anything about it. In other words, you have a right to an opinion about the way you would like your world to be. But when you don't do anything except moan and groan about it, that is merely unproductive complaining.

To not have anyone around you ruin your day with their complaining, you might want to establish a Complaint Free Zone either at home or at work and post this sign:

THIS IS A COMPLAINT FREE ZONE

If you want to complain, criticize or gossip,

please step away to somewhere else.

Lighten-Up

Office Sign:

SORRY,
YESTERDAY WAS THE DEADLINE
FOR ALL COMPLAINTS

DUMP THE GUNK

⌘

You must empty a box before you fill it again.

—IRISH SAYING

A UNIVERSITY PROFESSOR once visited a Japanese Zen master named Nanin to inquire about the teachings of Zen. Nanin treated his guest to a cup of tea. He poured the tea into a cup, and kept pouring even when the cup was full and overflowing. The professor watched until he could no longer restrain himself. "It is full to overflowing. No more will go in!" he said.

The Zen master replied, "Like this cup, you are full of your own opinions and speculations. How can I show you Zen unless you first empty your cup?"

Part of the sludge at the bottom of your cup, the stuff

that is weighing you down and ruining your day, could be because you are seeing your old annoyances, frustrations, and problems in the same way you have always seen them. Perhaps it is time to dump that gunk and see things in a new way. Many discoveries, in fact, are made because someone looked at something, which was annoying them, in a different way.

Netflix, for example, the online DVD rental company, was launched after one of its founders, Reed Hastings, was annoyed after having misplaced a videocassette he had rented and had to pay a large late fee. Later, as he was headed to the gym to exercise, he realized that the gym charged him one fee no matter how many times he went there or how long he used the equipment. This one-fee-for-unlimited-use idea became the model for Netflix—this very successful company where you pay one fee and keep the videos as long as you want.

Similar to the way Netflix was conceived, solutions to your "stuff" might be found in seeing it in a different way. Sometimes, when we get into an irritable mood, or in a rut, what our brain and body is telling us is that perhaps we need to do something differently, something that will refresh us, something that will put a spark back into our life.

In addition, we sometimes fill our life with so many things that we forget to leave room for what is really important. Perhaps this week would be a good time to examine what is in your cup. If it contains any negativity, uncertainty, or upsets, use some of the positive ideas in this book to get rid of them. Perhaps it is time to empty the things that have been annoying you. Perhaps it is time to pour out the bitterness in order to allow the sweeter things to take its place.

Follow-Up

Darkness is the only path to light. It is not our wonderful gifts that make us closer to God; it's using our garbage to transform ourselves.

—YEHUDA BERG,
author

Many years ago, I took a workshop from a Native American spiritual teacher. I don't remember her name but I do remember a simple powerful question she posed. She asked, "What do you do with your garbage?"

She meant it literally referring to how we are polluting the world with things we discard, things that take a long time to decay, things that will remain in garbage dumps for thousands of years. But when I now think about what she was asking, I also see that this could be viewed on a whole different level. The same question could be asked about what we do with our non-physical trash like our unkind thoughts or hurts we have caused to others, or even to ourselves.

This week might be a good time to get rid of your garbage, those mental things that are rotting and smelling up your life. Stop gathering evidence to prove that you are right and to make others wrong. It is time to realize that no one, no thing, and no circumstance is ruining your day. You are the only one who can do that.

To start the you-can't-ruin-my-day process, it might be good to empty your cup. Get rid of thoughts such as how the world is out to get you, how nothing is going your way, how everything is a continuous struggle. The truth is that everything is perfect, no one is out to get you, the world is full of prosperity, and you can do everything with ease and grace.

Lighten-Up

After I drink coffee I like to show the empty mug to the IT guy to tell him that I've successfully installed Java. He hates me.

—ANONYMOUS

CROSS THE STREET

⌘

If you're in a more negative mood, you're more likely to interact with someone else in a more negative way, and that person is more likely to interact in a negative way.

—JOHN CACIOPPO,
psychologist

A FRIEND OF mine once jokingly said that the initials for the television station CNN should stand for "Constant Negative News." Her witticism is probably not too far from the truth. Most news, after all, is pretty dreary these days.

We are constantly reminded of not-so-funny stuff—disasters, companies failing, Wall Street swindlers, bank robberies, neighborhood fires, people out of work, people dying, homelessness, shootings, senseless wars...the list goes on and on.

Yes, there is lots of negative stuff in the world, but that does not mean that you need to surround yourself with it. And yes, it is important to work to right the wrongs in the world, but it is also important to keep your balance while doing that good work. Focusing on the negative news, which we are constantly being bombarded with, is not productive or healthy, especially hearing those things the first thing in the morning or the last thing before bed.

I learned a related lesson a long time ago. Like turning off the frequently gloomy news, I can also get, what I call, the "voices of doom" people out of my life. It is those people who can easily ruin your day.

When I lived in New York City, I would walk my dog at least twice a day. During those walks, I would meet a woman who lived down the street. She was the most negative person I ever met. Nearly every day I would meet her and she would tell me about all the fights, fires, robberies, rapes, or police actions that happened in our neighborhood. I nicknamed her "The Voice of Doom."

I guess I'm a slow learner, but it took me months to realize that I didn't have to walk my dog in her direction. I could go the opposite way, not encounter her, and not hear all those depressing reports.

You, too, can start having a great day every day, by taking a different direction, crossing the street, and getting those "voices of doom" out of your life.

I no longer live in New York City but I still have a dog, albeit a different one. While walking my dog one morning where I now live, my neighbor asked if I watched the news last night. When I asked her why, she said that it totally depressed her and freaked her out. In fact, she was so upset that she had to take a tranquilizer. From her reaction to what she heard on the news, I thought that some earth-shattering event occurred.

But no it wasn't that. It was a graphic depiction of a dog that had been mistreated and beaten by its owner for five months. As a dog owner, it was disturbing to hear this but certainly not a major world event. I tried to calm her down and refocus her energy on the beautiful day it was, but she still went on and on about the news report.

My neighbor had a choice. She could continue to think about that mistreated animal, and let it ruin her day, or she could turn her attention elsewhere, perhaps even volunteering at an animal shelter to help battered dogs. But the point is, she chose to let that one incident, that one news report, ruin her day.

Bad things happen. Sometimes there is nothing we can do about it. But we can do something about how long, and how intensely, we focus on those events.

Follow-Up

*People deal too much with the negative, with what
is wrong. Why not try and see positive things, to just
touch those things and make them bloom?*

—THÍCH NHẤT HẠNH,
Zen Buddhist monk

My spouse and I have a friend who never makes up her mind.
If we invite her to a sit-down dinner party, she will say that
she is coming. Then she will call five or six times to say she
is not coming, then that she is coming. Then, maybe even
an hour before the dinner, she will say she's not coming.
We like her but her indecisiveness drives us nuts. So, after
bearing the brunt of her indecisions, we decided on how to
handle any future invitations we extend to her.

If it is an occasion that requires a firm commitment, we
do not invite her. If, on the other hand, it is a less formal
event, where it doesn't matter when or if guests arrive, we
invite her. We started this policy several years ago, and it
has worked well ever since. We are no longer upset by her
behavior, and it is much more pleasant when we see her.

You can handle your upsets in the same way. Make a
list of those "voices of doom" in your life—all those people
who upset you and ruin your day. Then, next to their name,
write down exactly what you will do to limit their presence
in your life. You don't have to actually get them out of your

life. But remember you have the power to change your reaction when other people annoy you. You can write down what action you will take so that those things will no longer have power over you.

Lighten-Up

A woman was at her salon getting her hair styled for a trip to Rome. She mentioned the trip to the hairdresser, who responded, "Rome? Why would anyone want to go there? It's crowded and dirty. You're crazy to go to Rome. So, how are you getting there?"

"We're taking Alitalia Airlines," was the reply. "We got a great rate!"

"Alitalia?" exclaimed the hairdresser. "That's not such a great airline. Their planes are old, their flight attendants are ugly, and they're often late. So, where will you be staying?"

"We'll be at this exclusive little place overlooking the Tiber River."

"Don't go any further. I know that place. It's really a dump."

"We're going to go see the Vatican and maybe get to see the Pope."

The hairdresser laughed. "You and a million others. He'll look the size of an ant. Good luck on this trip of yours. You're going to need it."

A month later, the woman again came in for a hairdo. The

hairdresser asked her about her trip to Rome.

"It was wonderful," explained the woman. "Not only were we on one of Alitalia's brand-new planes, but it was over-booked, and they gave us sleeper-seats in first class. The food and wine were wonderful. And the hotel was great! They'd just finished a million-dollar renovation, and now it's a jewel."

"Well," muttered the hairdresser, "that's all well and good, but I know you didn't get to see the Pope."

"Actually, we were quite lucky. As we toured the Vatican, a Swiss Guard tapped me on the shoulder. He explained that the Pope likes to meet some of the visitors, and if I'd be so kind as to step into his private room and wait, the Pope would personally greet me. Sure enough, five minutes later, the Pope walked through the door and shook my hand! I knelt down and he spoke a few words to me."

"Oh, really! What'd he say?"

He said, "Who gave you that hideous hairdo?"

MOVE YOUR FEAR
TO THE REAR

⌘

*Fear is the cheapest room in the house. I would like to
see you living in better conditions.*

—HAFIZ,
Persian poet

I ALMOST FAILED speech in college. I got a D in public
speaking. And my other grades were also low because of
my fear of speaking in front of a group. I was terrified to
raise my hand to ask or answer a question, even when I knew
the answer. Yet, for the past twenty-plus years I have had a
professional speaking career.

What changed?

For one thing, it was my passion to share my message.
After my wife's death, and seeing how her sense of humor

helped me get through those trying times, I devoted my life to teaching others about the therapeutic value of humor. To do this, I had to overcome my fear of public speaking.

Fear is a powerful force. It can be a signal of real danger. But more often than not, in most of today's modern society, the threat of dangerous incidents occurring is few and far between. It is our imagined fear that is the real danger. It prevents us from facing challenges in our life, from moving forward, and from doing the things we enjoy. Even the biggest names in the world have to deal with their fear. Did you know, for example, that Barbra Streisand did not perform in front of a live audience for over twenty years because of her performance anxiety?

Public speaking is supposedly one of the biggest fears people have. As a professional speaker, do I get nervous when I get up to speak? You are darn right I do. But I've learned to focus on my message and a positive outcome. I am determined not to let the fear get in my way. The most important thing I learned was that I could feel the fear and do it anyway.

Fear can also ruin our day in other ways too. We have fears that we are not good enough, so we don't present our best self to the world. We fear that we might do something wrong or make a mistake, so we don't do or say something. We fear that we won't get a certain job, so we don't even apply for it.

But our fears are not always real. They often originate in our mind from past experiences or conditioning. I, for example, grew up in a predominantly Jewish neighborhood in the Bronx. I was taught to look down on anyone who wasn't Jewish, people who didn't do or act as we did. The ironic and unfortunate thing about this, however, was that there were a lot of other non-Jews who were teaching their children the same thing, only this time it was against us.

Such upbringing only separated us from the rest of the world. Despite a popular phrase that says, "When you're in love, the whole world is Jewish," it wasn't. Such teachings caused me to fear people of other ethnic backgrounds, or those who spoke a different language than I did or those who had a different skin color. I am still trying to move some of those deep-seated fears to the rear so that I can fully appreciate other people.

~~~~~~~~~~~~~~~~~~~~~~

False Fears

I once heard someone say that the acronym for FEAR is False Evidence Appearing Real. I love that because often many of our fears are non-existent in the real world. They are simply in our mind. And those false fears can not only ruin our day but also ruin our life.

One great example of encountering a false fear comes from an organization that uses a simple test in their training. Each small group is given an easy task—to follow a wilderness trail for one mile, touch a white fence that crosses the path at the one-mile marker, and return to the training center.

Prior to the mission's start, the groups are told to stay alert, as there are water moccasins and alligators in the area. Both can be dangerous and are sometimes on the path. A stern reminder is again given to complete the mission, "Touch the white fence and return in under eighteen minutes." A final warning is made before starting: "We have wild boars in Florida, and they are mean and aggressive. If you see a wild boar, take appropriate action, but complete the mission!"

What the participants don't know is that half a mile into the run, a staff member is hidden in the brush ready to make the sound of a wild boar. The response of the runners is captured on video, and it almost always produces pure terror. They immediately turn around and sprint back to the training center in complete panic. When they arrive, the trainers ask just one question, "Did you complete the mission?" The explanation they offer for their failure is, "We heard something."

What the participants heard was real. But what they thought it was, was in their heads. Those false fears colored their thinking and blocked their completing the assigned task.

~~~~~~~~~~~~~~~~~~~~~~~~~~~

Follow-Up

If your mind is in a loving place...your experience will reflect that. If your mind is in a fearful place...your experience will reflect that.

—MARIANNE WILLIAMSON,
author and speaker

This week it's time to examine your fears and see how they are impacting you, and perhaps ruining your day. List a few of your fears and then ask yourself: Where did these fears come from? Are they real? Are they necessary? Are they contributing to or diminishing the enjoyment of my life?

If you want to have a great day, you need to confront those fears. Then do what you have to do in spite of them.

I encourage you to start with your small fears and then move on to your bigger ones. You might also want to keep a journal this week as you investigate a specific fear. Take note of your sensations, thoughts, emotions, and beliefs about that fear.

When you write down your fears, you bring that fear forward in your consciousness. Instead of saying, "I don't want to talk about it," you can examine various aspects of it. In the process that fear might even start to go away.

When I took the est Training, I remember a process we did to relieve any pain that we were experiencing. If you had a headache, for example, you would fully investigate the pain by asking yourself such questions as, "How far to the left is it?" "How far to the right?" "How deep in my head is it?" "How far down from the top of my head is it?" "Which side of my head was it closer to, left or right?" "What size is it?" "What shape is it?" "What color is it?" etc.

I now realize that what the process was doing was identifying exactly what the pain looked like and bringing it into my consciousness. In doing so, the pain often went away.

Closely examining your fears could also make them less prominent in your life.

Lighten-Up

They say people are more afraid of public speaking than they are of snakes.

It doesn't seem to make sense. I mean, you don't see someone walking through the desert, suddenly shouting, "Watch out, a podium!"

—ANONYMOUS

PART THREE

GROW-UP (NOT!)

When I grow up
What would I like to be?
That's what grown-ups
Are always asking me.

If I could go into the future,
See what's ahead of me,
Maybe then I would know
Just what I want to be.

So I traveled fifty years ahead
In an incredible time machine,
And now let me tell you
Exactly what I've seen.

I was old, and bald, and wrinkly,
A hearing aid in my left ear.
My belly was growing by the moment,
And I had a big, fat rear.

I was busy paying mortgages,
Taxes and other bills.
I worried about my health,
And took lots of medicine pills.

Well, now I know what I want to be,
And it may sound wild...
But more than anything, when I grow up,
I'd like to be a child.

—ALAN GETTIS,
"The Incredible Time Machine,"
from the book *In the Beak of a Duck*

GROW DOWN
TO LIGHTEN UP

⌘

All children, except one, grow up. They soon know that they will grow up, and the way Wendy knew was this. One day when she was two years old she was playing in a garden, and she plucked another flower and ran with it to her mother. I suppose she must have looked rather delightful, for Mrs. Darling put her hand to her heart and cried, 'Oh, why can't you remain like this for ever!' This was all that passed between them on the subject, but henceforth Wendy knew that she must grow up. You always know after you are two. Two is the beginning of the end.

—J. M. BARRIE,
The Adventures of Peter Pan

TODAY, YOU MAY encounter someone who angers you or some problem that seems unsolvable. Instead of carrying that around with you, I'd like to suggest you might get some new insights into that issue by considering how a child might deal with it. Yes, I said a child because children possess unencumbered wisdom.

Actor Dom DeLuise, for example, noted in a magazine interview, "I've had a couple of serious bouts with depression where nothing made me laugh. Everything was wrong—life was hopeless and I was feeling useless. One of the best gifts I ever got was at Christmastime one year when I was depressed. When my son asked me what I wanted for Christmas, I said, 'Happiness—and you can't give it to me.' On Christmas day, this little innocent boy who weighed sixty pounds gave me a piece of cardboard with the word 'Happiness' written on it. He simply said, 'You see, Dad, I can give you happiness!'"

Children's book author and illustrator Maurice Sendak recounts another charming story about one child's unbridled enthusiasm:

"Once a little boy sent me a charming card with a little drawing. I loved it. I answer all my children's letters—sometimes very hastily—but this one I lingered over. I sent him a card and I drew a picture of a Wild Thing on it. I wrote, 'Dear Jim: I loved your card.'

"Then I got a letter back from his mother and she said, 'Jim loved your card so much he ate it.'

"That to me was one of the highest compliments

I've ever received. He didn't care that it was an original Maurice Sendak drawing or anything. He saw it, he loved it, he ate it."

Adults carry with them a whole history of past experiences that frequently color their decisions of their current circumstances. Children, on the other hand, don't have that background that might influence their actions. They therefore often provide a much more spontaneous and clearer take on a situation.

Young children are not spoiled by the complexities of the adult world. They often cut right through adult limited thinking. They get right to the heart of the matter. Sometimes their unadulterated wisdom can provide much more direct and simple answers to problems.

The Sky's the Limit

A horoscope I once read contained a powerful story illustrating the unlimited thinking of children. Astrologer Rob Brezsny wrote, "It was Take Our Daughter to Work Day recently. I brought my five-year-old Taurus sprite Zoe to my command center. 'Do you want to be like Daddy when you grow up and write stories for people?' I asked as I showed her around my empire of words. 'No. Too much sitting around,' she said. 'So tell me what you'd like to be.' His daughter answered, 'A dancer-clown-doctor who drives bulldozers.'"

Adults limit themselves. They make excuses why something can't be accomplished—"It's raining out," "I'm too old," "It will be too crowded." While some reasons may be valid, often they are not. Children, on the other hand, embrace all possibilities. In the eyes of a child anything is possible, even being a "dancer-clown-doctor who drives bulldozers."

You can gain much by learning to embrace anything-is-possible childlike thinking. Yes, anything is possible, even not letting anything ruin your day.

Follow-Up

If I'm very depressed or if something's bothering me today, my husband, Larry, and I go back to the park. We get on the carousel horse and we start riding, and I start singing at the top of my lungs. It is pure and absolute joy and happiness.

—EDA LESHAN,
writer

If you are dealing with a trying situation, ask a child how they might handle it. Their answer may not actually help you solve your problem but often it will give you a chuckle and perhaps help you view your situation from a fresh and new angle.

On the other hand, the way children act could provide you with some things you might do to ease a situation. For example, children throw a temper tantrum when they are upset. If you are angry with someone, you might do the same. Jump up and down shouting, "They're not going to change and there's nothing I can do about it." "They're not going to change and there's nothing I can do about it." "They're not going to change and there's nothing I can do about it."

Young children discharge their energy by running around a lot. Maybe you need to go to the track or the gym to release any negative energy you are harboring.

Children take a nap when they get overly tired and cranky. Maybe you need a nap too when you get irritable.

Today, ask yourself: "What would a child do to not let their situation ruin their day?"

Lighten-Up

I was testing children in my Dublin Sunday school class to see if they understood the concept of getting to heaven.

I asked them, "If I sold my house and my car, had a big garage sale and gave all my money to the church, would that get me into heaven?"

"NO!" the children answered.

"If I cleaned the church every day, mowed the garden, and kept everything tidy, would that get me into heaven?"

Again, the answer was "NO!"

"If I gave sweets to all the children and loved my husband, would that get me into heaven?"

Again, they all answered "NO!"

I was just bursting with pride for them.

I continued, "Then how can I get into heaven?"

A six-year-old boy shouted out: "Yuv gotta be fookin' dead..."

DON'T WORRY, BE HAPPY

⌘

When I wake up in the morning I have two choices. I can be happy or I can be unhappy. I'm not an idiot, I choose to be happy.

—NORMAN VINCENT PEALE,
minister and author

IF YOU ARE going on a trip, the first thing you need to decide is where you want to go. Without that you will never reach a destination. Your daily journey is no different. The first step to getting where you want to go, or to changing where you are, is to align yourself with what you want to happen. You can set out to have a happy day or not. The choice is yours.

An example from my own life happened several years ago.

I was on the road for a speaking engagement and it was my birthday. I was not pleased having to spend this special day in an unfamiliar city with a group of strangers. So, I decided to change that and set my intention to have a fun birthday by myself in spite of not being with friends or family.

That morning, during my presentation, I let my audience know that it was my birthday. I told them that as a gift I would like a hug from each of them. I not only got hugs throughout the day but throughout the several-day conference as well.

Later on, in the crowded hotel elevator, I announced my birthday and asked twelve total strangers to sing "Happy Birthday." What a wonderfully funny sight it was to see people singing "Happy Birthday" as I exited the closing doors.

Next, I headed to buy myself flowers. After I selected some lilies, I asked the florist if she had a card to include with them. She handed me one and then, noticing how much thought and care I was taking in writing it, asked, "Are you buying these for someone special." "Yes," I said, "me." She looked puzzled and then laughed as I wrote, "To Allen, Happy Birthday. I love you." And then I signed my name.

What I noticed throughout the day was that everyone I told that it was my birthday—from the hassled hotel desk clerk, who gave me a vase for my flowers, to the convenience store clerk, who looked like she hadn't smiled for years—all brightened up, became friendly, and helped me celebrate.

Would my day have been as joyful without my intention

for it to be so? Probably not but who knows? What I do know is that setting my intention to create a happy day for myself certainly didn't hurt.

~~~~~~~~~~~~~~~~~~~~~~~~~~~

Create the Day You Want

Several years ago, I received an email from someone I had never met before. I almost didn't open it because I didn't recognize the address. Then, I nearly deleted it because I thought it was one of those spam emails from Nigeria. You know the kind: All I had to do was send them money, and they would transfer millions into my bank account.

I was especially skeptical because the first sentence read: "I'm just writing to inform you that my girlfriend and I have named a holiday after you." Sure, I thought. And how much will that cost me? But I read on:

"I'm hoping that you won't be offended as it is a very nice holiday, one that symbolizes the love that we have for each other. It's just that the day is named after you, nothing more."

I get lots of loony email. Most are annoying but this one sounded intriguing, so I kept reading.

"Allow me to explain. My girlfriend and I work together in a business with long hours. On our first Valentine's Day together, we worked past midnight, and so missed the holiday. Rather than get depressed, we decided that from then on, we would celebrate the next day (February 15th) as 'Allen Klein's Day.'"

How could I not read further after being chosen for such an honor?

"Yes, I know it is sort of a pun—perhaps the lowest form of humor—but it was a pun between us, and we don't mind laughing at puns in private. Go ahead, say the words out loud, 'Valentine's Day,' 'Allen Klein's Day.' Get it?

"Anyway, as the holiday named in your honor is fast approaching, I thought I'd do a quick web search to find out the true identity of its patron. And, as luck would have it, you happened to be the first—and therefore in my book, the only—Allen Klein I found.

"Honestly, sir, I know the whole thing is a bit strange, but I just figured you had a right to know if a holiday had your name on it. I wanted you to be privy to the fact that come February 15th, two young lovers—complete strangers to you—will kiss over candlelight, raise a glass, and toast in all sincere sweetness to each other: 'Happy Allen Klein's Day.'"

~~~~~~~~~~~~~~~~~~~~~~~~~~

Follow-Up

Beliefs have the power to create and the power to destroy. Human beings have the awesome ability to take any experience of their lives and create a meaning that disempowers them or one that can literally save their lives.

—TONY ROBBINS,
author and speaker

Sam Berns had a rare early-aging disease called progeria. Sam, who was the subject of an HBO documentary, died recently at the age of seventeen. When asked by an interviewer before his death, "What is the most important thing people should know about you?" Sam replied, "I have a very happy life."

Sam's reasons for saying that were threefold. First, he focused on what he could do, not on what he couldn't. Second, he surrounded himself with people who were caring and loving. And third, he kept moving forward.

When life hands you things that you don't want or didn't ask for, perhaps you should follow Sam's advice and choose to be happy by focusing on three things: Find something you can do in a situation to make it better instead of blaming someone else. Surround yourself with positive, uplifting people instead of those who find fault with the way things are. And, finally, instead of looking back at harm someone might have caused you, or an unhappy situation, move forward and choose to be happy.

If you have been putting off being happy until you pay off your mortgage, until your kids go to college, until you win the lottery, then you may never be happy. Realize the only time you have is now. There really isn't any tomorrow until it comes. So if you want happiness, don't wait. Choose it now.

You make hundreds of decisions every day. From the moment you get out of bed, you are deciding what to wear, what to have for breakfast, will you go to the gym, etc. Well, make one more decision starting today—decide to be happy today and every day.

In other words, you can be happy right now, no matter what.

Lighten-Up

If you can start the day without caffeine,

If you can always be cheerful, ignoring aches and pains,

If you can resist complaining and boring people with your troubles,

If you can eat the same food every day and be grateful for it,

If you can understand when your loved ones are too busy to give you any time,

If you can take criticism and blame without resentment,

If you can conquer tension without medical help,
If you can relax without alcohol,
If you can sleep without the aid of drugs,
Then you are probably...
The family dog.

LET THE PLAY BEGIN

⌘

Play is one of the most powerful ways of breaking up
hopelessness and bringing energy into a situation.

—O. CARL SIMONTON,
oncologist

IF YOU ARE upset, angry, or frustrated with anyone, or anything, you cannot laugh about it. One of the quickest ways to change that, and get more laughter and less stress in a situation, is to start to let go of it with play. It changes your energy toward the things that annoy you. It allows you to see what is happening without getting entangled in it. And it does so in a fun and lighthearted way.

When you were a child, chances are you had things you really enjoyed doing. Things you loved to play with. If you were a girl, perhaps it was dressing up your dolls or dressing yourself up. If you were a boy, maybe it was playing baseball or trading sports cards.

One of my favorite things was to make believe that I was a deliveryman. I'd ride my oversized metal moving van up and down the long hallway in our apartment. I'd load the truck up with my toys on one end of the hallway and deliver them down at the other end. Then I would repeat the process for many hours.

All of us have favorite things we did as a child. As an adult, you probably can no longer do some of those things, like riding a toy truck at work. But others, like perhaps dressing up from time to time, you might be able to get back into your life again.

"When we get grown up," says Liz McKechnie of Aspire Leadership, "it's easy to forget what fun we had and how we learned new things and came up with new ideas when we were kids."

We also forget that children can be our greatest play teachers.

One day while waiting to board a plane, an announcement came over the loudspeaker: "Ladies and gentlemen. We are sorry to inform you that, because of mechanical problems, your flight will be delayed. The mechanics are headed to the aircraft and we will inform you of their progress as soon as we can."

The adults in the area moaned and groaned about the situation. Some went up to the counter to complain. Then

I noticed a couple of kids who responded to the situation much differently. For them, the delay was an opportunity to play. They sat down on the carpet, took out their miniature toy cars, and proceeded to use the pattern in the rug as a superhighway for their game.

Author and theologian, Michael Yaconelli, reminds us the true value of play for adults when dealing with a difficult world. He says, "Play is not an escape; it is the way to release the life-smothering grip of busyness, stress, and anxiety."

Playing with Rejection

Bernie De Koven, a colleague and friend of mine, counteracted a mountain of rejection slips he was getting from publishers by playing with the situation. He wrote his own rejection slip and sent it back to them. He called it, "A rejection slip rejection."

It read: "The author regrets that he is unable to accept the enclosed rejection slip. This in no way reflects on the quality of the rejection, but rather on the author's needs at the present time. Signed, The author."

De Koven says, "I had five hundred printed, on cardstock, with an embossed frame. From then on, I returned the rejection slips to the publisher, with my rejection slip attached and actually heard back from a couple of them, with handwritten apologies, no less."

Follow-Up

Every good journey needs a GPS system. Not a global positioning satellite but a Gotta Play Some system. Whatever pressures, demands, expectations, and heartache we have in our lives, we need to take time out to play.

—SCOTT FRIEDMAN,
keynote speaker

In my longer workshops, I ask the audience to participate in a playful process to help them reframe their stress. Each group, of about five to seven people, is given a bag of assorted props that include such unrelated things as a hotel-sized bar of soap, a lollipop, a greeting card, a ping-pong ball, a straw, a whistle, etc. Each bag has about eight items in it, and each is totally different from the other.

I ask the group to decide on what stresses them out the most. That is what they will work on (or play with). I then instruct them to put all the props out where everyone in the group can see them. Next, I have them make up a story about the thing that stresses them out using the props and with the following guidelines: The story could be as long or short as they want. The same prop can be used more than once in the story. It is not necessary to use every prop.

The results are amazing. When the stories are recited back, people are laughing hysterically when the thing that stresses them out is told in a playful context using the props.

You might want to try this too either at work, perhaps to start a meeting, or by yourself, gathering a handful of items around your house, or at work. However you proceed, remember that play is a powerful way to reframe the rough spots in your life.

Lighten-Up

There are children playing in the street who could solve some of my top problems in physics, because they have modes of sensory perception that I lost long ago.

—J. ROBERT OPPENHEIMER,
physicist

A little boy was waiting for his mother to come out of the grocery store. As he waited, a man approached him and asked, "Son, can you tell me where the post office is?"

The little boy replied, "Sure! Just go straight down this street a couple blocks and turn to your right."

The man thanked the boy kindly and said, "I'm the new pastor in town. I'd like for you to come to church on Sunday. I'll show you how to get to Heaven."

The little boy replied with a chuckle, "You're kidding me, right? You don't even know the way to the post office!"

GET THEE TO A TOY STORE

⌘

I collect stuffed animals,
and toy stores make me happy.

—GRACE SLICK,
singer

MANY ADULTS THINK that toy stores are just for kids. The truth is that they are wonderful resources for adults, especially if you are down in the dumps or need to offset something that has ruined your day. Practically anything you find in a toy store, except perhaps for toy soldiers and fake guns, can be a reminder to lighten up.

In addition, if you need to find a solution to a vexing problem, "goofing off" or relaxing with a toy can help you accomplish that. As an example of the benefits of taking time-out, philosopher Eric Hoffer points out, "It is leisure, not work, that produces the most important inventions. Many inventions had their birth as toys, and such critical instruments as the telescope and microphone were first conceived as playthings."

Also, toys that evoke amusement or laughter can be a fun way to release tension, combat stress, and help you brighten up your day. A few well-chosen wind-up toys jumping around your desk, for instance, can immediately change your mood. Or, when they are scattered around the boardroom table, they can change the entire atmosphere of a boring meeting.

An additional benefit of a toy is that it can draw you and someone else together as you both reminisce about your favorite childhood toy or share how you both like the one you might be playing with now.

Several years ago I saw the power of what a simple toy could do. It was when my mom was in a rehab hospital recuperating from a broken hip. I brought her a hand puppet, which looked exactly like a life-sized golden retriever puppy. A lot of the patients in the wing had dementia or Alzheimer's. Many sat and stared at the wall or, looking glum, held their head in their hands. But when I wheeled my mom and the animated puppet around the facilities, suddenly faces regained their spirits and lit up with smiles and laughter.

Another example of the power of a toy comes from Nikki Stone, an Olympic gold medal winner in the sport of inverted aerial skiing. What makes her story so remarkable is that, just two years before her win, doctors said that she would never ski again due to unrecoverable damage to two of her spinal discs.

Stone says, "When my doctor told me I was going to have to push through agonizing pain if I was ever to get back to jumping again, I knew I needed some external focus to remind me to keep my tough outer shell."

She got that encouragement from a toy—a small rubber Super Ball. Throughout her painful ordeal it reminded her that, like the ball, she had a hard outer shell, that she could stay strong and that she could bounce back. This simple toy helped her achieve, and stay focused on, her goal.

Toys were a big deal when we were young. We learned a lot about our world by playing with them. Toys can be valuable assets for adults too. Not only can they bring us joy, but they can also help us see our stress and struggles in a lighter way.

~~~~~~~~~~~~~~~~~~~~~~~~~~~

Corporate Fun

Some major companies are realizing that creating an environment with a fun atmosphere not only helps with creativity but also with the bottom line. If people enjoy where they work, they will work harder, be more productive, and stay with a company longer. In other words, workers who play together, stay together.

Google's Manhattan offices are a prime example of such a company. They provide a fun atmosphere, where some employees create their own workspaces. One cubicle, for example, has cutout claw-footed bathtubs repurposed into couches. Another looks like a vintage subway car.

In addition, toys and games can be found throughout Google's headquarters. There is a hallway arcade, a game/exercise room with pool tables and table hockey, and scooters to traverse the five acres of space it occupies in the Chelsea section of New York City.

~~~~~~~~~~~~~~~~~~~~~~~~

Follow-Up

Give in to the power of goofiness. It lets the mind relax and catch its breath. Only goofiness has the inherent power to keep seriousness from killing off all your ideas. Ripples of laughter will wash up the brightest gems on the shore of your consciousness.

—DALTON ROBERTS,
columnist

This week, visit a toy store. Look around and see what calls out to you. What brings a smile to your face? What tickles your funny bone? Perhaps it's a wacky wind-up toy, a kooky-looking stuffed animal, or a cute, cuddly teddy bear. Buy a few of your favorites. Then try and interact with them every day.

If nothing else, they will help to remind you to lighten up. They can help you see things more playfully, perhaps with a new perspective, perhaps less seriously. And, depending on the cuddliness of the toy, they can also bring reassurance in unsettling times. As Susan Schwartz, teddy bear collector and author of *Teddy Bear Philosophy*, says, "At times when we are stressed out, toys instantly bring us back to times when we felt loved and comforted."

Lighten-Up

When I was a kid, I went to the store and asked the guy, "Do you have any toy train schedules?"

—STEVEN WRIGHT,
comedian

A boy and his father are playing with toy cars. The father has the police car and pretends to pull over the car that the boy is playing with.

"Do you have a driver's license?" asks the father.

"No," says the boy.

"Are you resisting arrest?" he asks.

The boy hesitates before he says, "No, but I'm not sleepy at all."

(Get it? No? Then look at the next to the last line again—"...resisting a rest?" Now do you get it?)

MAKE IT A RED NOSE DAY

⌘

When you put on a clown suit and a rubber nose,
nobody has any idea what you look like inside.

—STEPHEN KING,
author

I AM A big fan of a little red sponge-rubber ball known as a "clown nose." It is near impossible not to smile when you either see someone wearing one or when you are wearing one yourself.

Over the past twenty years, I have given an envelope with a clown nose hidden inside to everyone in my workshops and at my keynote speeches. I then ask them to close their eyes and think about something that is upsetting them or even some physical ache or pain they may be having.

After a minute or so, I ask them to open the packet, put on the clown nose, and look around the room.

The smiles and laughter flood the room as the upsets they recall, or the discomfort they felt, disappear. In addition, I ask the audience to take the clown nose with them and use it in stressful situations. The tales that have come back are amazing.

I personally saw the power of a clown nose when my flight was three hours late in taking off. I gave one to the flight attendant who was greeting people as they entered the aircraft. Most of the passengers were grumpy and unresponsive when she smiled and said "Hello." But when she put on the clown nose many of the passengers smiled and lit up. Interestingly, not all of the passengers were cheered up by it. A few people immediately turned away preferring to hang on to their anger.

Recently, there was a New York-based designer named Ji Lee who put red clown noses on posters all around the city. His goal was to add a little levity to the often-serious world of advertising. Using what he called "Clownify Stickers," Lee turned billboard models into clever works of art simply by putting removable clown nose stickers to their picture-perfect faces.

Lee told the Huffington Post, "There are lots of ads everywhere, so I wondered how I can make my commute a little bit more fun for me and for everyone around.... When I place these stickers, people often laugh and give me a 'thumb up' [sic]. I think people enjoy them."

One ad for the HBO series *Silicon Valley* was renamed "Silly-clown Valley" after Lee added the red noses to the five faces of the actors. Other somber ads, like a gun-slinging Liam Neeson in the film *Non-Stop*, or a grimacing young woman struggling to lift weights in a gym ad, suddenly took on a whole new aura.

While this project may border on graffiti, which I strongly dislike because it ruins other people's property, in my opinion this playful undertaking somehow enhanced the advertising instead of destroying it. Lee showed us how a simple clown nose could transform something that had the intent of being serious into something joyful. He noted, "Ads are definitely more fun with clowns in them."

You can take a hint from Lee. To paraphrase him, "Life's predicaments can definitely be more fun, and less stressful, with clowns in them."

Saving Someone's Life

For several years in a row, my daughter Sarah was a counselor at Camp Tawonga near Yosemite National Park. Every year she would ask me to come and speak to her fellow counselors about the power of humor. And every year I would make some kind of excuse—I'm too busy, it's a long drive, it's too hot up there.

Then I heard a fellow speaker give a powerful

talk. One of the things he mentioned was that teenagers have the highest rate of suicide in this country. His words moved me. I immediately left his talk, called Sarah and asked, "When do you want me to come and address the teenage counselors?"

When I arrived Sarah informed me that I would be speaking at eleven o'clock at night after all the campers had gone to bed. As I started my talk, I scanned the room looking for a friend of Sarah's who was also a counselor. He was very shy, and from her description, often very depressed. I didn't see him in the room at first but during the program I spotted him crouched down behind the couch. His head would pop up every now and then.

Around midnight the talk was over. I searched for Sarah's friend but he quickly disappeared. Months later I ran into him on the street. Usually he would hardly acknowledge me but this time he immediately came over and was eager to share something.

It seems that several days after my talk, he decided to leave the camp. He wasn't getting along with the other counselors. And since he no longer spoke to his mom or dad, he couldn't go home. So he decided to leave it up to fate and began hitchhiking.

For hours, car after car passed him by. As each one did, he felt more and more depressed and deserted. He started to plan how he would kill himself. Then, as it was getting dark, he put his hand in his pocket and the clown nose I gave out in my presentation fell out. He bent down and put it on. Immediately someone stopped to give him a ride.

"Maybe lightening up a bit can get me further than I thought," he said. "Thank you for coming to speak to us—and thank you for saving my life."

~~~~~~~~~~~~~~~~~~~~~~~~~~~

Follow-Up

Clowns wear a face that's painted intentionally on them so they appear to be happy or sad. What kind of mask are you wearing today?

—ANONYMOUS

What are you going to wear this week that is festive, fanciful, or fun? It is a great opportunity to experiment and dress up in some way, even if it is nothing more than with a playful tie, a wildly patterned blouse, or a pair of brightly colored underwear. Any of those could lift your spirit but to accelerate your disposition I highly recommend you get your own red clown nose.

Keep it handy when you are in traffic jams, use it at staff meetings when things get bogged down, or put one on to fend off arguments before they even get started.

And, if you are too embarrassed to wear a clown nose in public, wear one privately. Start each morning by putting on the nose, looking in the mirror, and saying out loud, "This person is not to be taken seriously."

Lighten-Up

In my humor and healing keynote presentations, I do an exercise with red clown noses. Everyone in the audience gets a sealed packet with one inside. With their eyes closed, I ask audience members to think of some difficulty they are having and then, still with their eyes closed, to open the packet and put on the clown nose. Then I ask them to open their eyes and look around the room.

I was a little reluctant to do this activity, however, when I addressed the annual meeting of the National Coalition for Cancer Survivorship. I knew that a number of people in the group had facial cancer. Some had only a partial nose, some none at all.

I checked with the meeting planner to make sure that the clown-nose process was appropriate. She assured me that even those with facial disfigurement would love it. Still, I was uncomfortable about doing it. My fears were quickly alleviated, however, when the group not only responded with overwhelming laughter but also delighted in sharing stories with me about their prosthetic noses.

One woman joyfully showed me a Polaroid photo taken

in her hotel room minutes before my speech. She told me that she was getting ready to attend my talk and proceeded to put adhesive glue on her prosthetic nose. Then she waited for it to dry. When it came time to attach the nose, however, it was gone. She could not find it. At that moment a friend knocked on the door. So she asked her friend to help locate it. The nose was finally found and a picture taken. It showed the nose stuck to the rear end of her slacks.

She delighted in telling me the story and in explaining the photo. But she was even more elated with her new clown nose. She said, "This is great. From now on, I have a choice of which nose to wear."

PART FOUR

CRACK-UP

*The beauty of using humor and keeping a sense of
lightness and playfulness in our life is that it helps us
deal with life as it is—the ups and downs,
the unexpected changes, and the frustrations
we may encounter.*

—KAREN HORNEFFER-GINTER,
psychologist and author

KEEP IT LIGHT

⌘

I have been confronted with many difficulties
throughout the course of my life, and my country is
going through a critical period. But I laugh often, and
my laughter is contagious. When people ask me how
I find the strength to laugh now, I reply that I am a
professional laugher.

—DALAI LAMA,
spiritual leader

WHEN I WAS growing up there were different approaches
to laughter in our home. My dad didn't laugh out loud much
and my mom laughed a lot. Even in her later years, she
used humor as one of the ways she coped with not-so-funny
situations.

In later years, for example, when she needed a walker to help her get around, she named it "Fred Astaire." Whenever there was live music at the independent living facility where she lived, she used it as her partner to dance around the multipurpose room.

I believe that our permission to laugh as an adult is greatly influenced by our childhood upbringing. Often children are told, "Wipe that smirk off your face," "Settle down," "Get serious." Still, if your teachers, parents, or other family members didn't allow for much laughter in your childhood, that doesn't mean you can't change that in your adulthood. Simply have some humorous reminders around, things that will help you to remember to lighten up and not let anyone ruin your day.

For example, I'm sitting in my office and looking around the room. What do I see? I see my computer, a printer, a telephone, and an assortment of books, folders, and papers. I also see a lot of things that bring a smile to my face and a laugh to my heart. I see a rubber chicken hanging on the door, a big red sign on the closet that says "Toys," a plaque made of wood hanging on the doorknob that reads "Play Zone." Another sign says, "Handicap: Bald Headed Parking Only." I also see several Teletubbies™ stuffed toys, a Woody Allen signed photo, a couple of red clown noses, and some funny family photos, among other humorous things.

As mentioned elsewhere, we are often surrounded by grouchy grumps, maddening moments, and negative news. We can let them get us down or we can rise above them. Lighthearted, uplifting, and funny "stuff" can help us instantly do just that.

One other thing about lightening up is that laughter can be mightier than the sword. It may seem a little strange suggesting that laughter can quell conflict. Yet throughout history there have been examples of this. One of them that I like best happened during the Cuban missile crisis when Soviet and American negotiators became deadlocked. There they sat in silence, until someone suggested that each person tell a humorous story. One of the Russians told a riddle: "What is the difference between capitalism and communism?" The answer? "In capitalism, man exploits man. In communism, it's the other way around."

The tactic worked; with the mood relaxed, the talks continued.

There are two reasons why humor and laughter are such powerful tools in a conflict. The first is that it gives you power over any unsettling or powerless situation. Since you might not be able to physically do anything about the encounter, it gives you mental superiority and the upper hand by laughing at it.

The second reason is that humor disarms your opponent. It catches them off guard. They are not used to a humorous attack and are at a loss of how to defend themselves.

An excellent example of both of these comes from the Chinese artist Ai Weiwei (pronounced EYE Way-way). His political pranks against the Communist Party have caused him to be severely beaten and put in prison; his studio was destroyed. But, in spite of all of this, he continues to produce provocative artwork that criticizes the government and draws worldwide attention. One YouTube video, for example, which parodies the Chinese state, shows him handcuffed while doing a Korean "Gangnam Style" dance.

The more the dictatorial government pushes, the more outspoken and the more playfully irreverent Weiwei's artwork becomes. In a reaction to the authorities installing fifteen cameras to monitor his every move and to his being blocked from traveling abroad, Weiwei posted a public "weiweicom" on the Internet directly from his bedroom. He says grinningly, "They almost begged me to turn it off."

Weiwei proves the power that humor can have. He says, "I think they [the Communist government] don't know how to handle someone like me. They kind of give up managing me."

The Humor Advantage

A young man at a construction site always bragged that he was stronger than everyone else there. He would especially make fun of one of the older work-men. After a while, the older man had had enough. "Why don't you put your money where your mouth is?" he said. "I'll bet you a week's pay that I can haul something in a wheelbarrow over to that building that you won't be able to wheel back."

"You're on," the braggart replied. "Let's see what you got."

The old man reached out and grabbed the wheelbarrow by the handles. Then, nodding to the young man, he said with a smile, "All right. Get in."

～～～～～～～～～

Follow-Up

Isn't it time that every physician asked us, as part of a regular physical exam, if we're having any fun? What's the point of having low cholesterol, low blood pressure, and good blood sugar if you're a miserable wretch?

—LORETTA LAROCHE,
author and speaker

There are three things that can help you lighten up. The first is to have *something* around to help you do that. The second is to have *someone* around to help you do that. And the third is not to take yourself so seriously.

We have already talked about having some toys, props, and other reminders around to lighten up your day. If you already have some of those, great, if not, get some. Put them in prominent places around your office or your home. They will act as prompts to not let anyone ruin your day and to lighten up any maddening moments you may encounter this week.

Second, find out who helps you lighten up and surround yourself with those people. They can be family, friends, acquaintances, coworkers, colleagues, etc. They can even be from the world of professional comics and cartoonists. It doesn't matter. What matters is that you keep those people in your arsenal of "humor buddies" that you can call upon to lift you up when things are getting you down.

I learned a lesson about the third item, not taking myself so seriously, at the beginning of my speaking career. I was hired to do a post-dinner presentation for surgeons and their spouses. After signing the contract, I found out that it was going to be a formal event. Since I had no tuxedo at the time, I went to Costco and bought one for ninety-nine dollars. I lucked out because it was the week prior to New Year's Eve. It didn't do so well, however, during the speech.

The tux had some weird side buckles that I apparently didn't fasten too well. During the program, one buckle came undone. Then the other side did too. I leaned to my left and caught the falling pants with my elbow. And that is the way I remained during the rest of the talk...one hand holding the microphone and the other arm holding up my pants.

I was too new in the speaking business to realize that I could have openly shared what was happening with the audience, instead of trying to hide it. Had I taken the situation less seriously and revealed my dilemma, I probably would have gotten a chance to buckle up again and maybe even get a great big laugh from the audience.

Lighten-Up

So I'm at the pet store buying a bag of dog food for my dog. While in the checkout line, a woman behind me asked if I had a dog. Why else would I be buying dog food, right? So on impulse I told her that no, I didn't have a dog; I said I was starting the dog food diet again, and that I probably shouldn't because I ended up in the hospital last time. Then, I said that I'd lost fifty pounds before I awakened in intensive care with tubes coming out of most of my orifices and IVs in both arms.

I told her that it was essentially a perfect diet. All you do is load your pockets with the nuggets and simply eat one or two every time you feel hungry. The food is nutritionally complete so it works well and I was going to try it again. (I have to mention here that practically everyone in line was now enthralled with my story.)

Horrified, she asked if I ended up in intensive care because the dog food poisoned me. I told her no, I stepped off a curb to sniff a poodle's butt and a car hit me. I thought the guy behind her was going to have a heart attack because he was laughing so hard.

OPEN YOUR HUMOR EYES

⌘

From there to here and here to there,
funny things are everywhere.

—DR. SEUSS,
author

A FRIEND OF mine, who attended my birthday party, told me what happened after she left the event. She said:

"At one point during the party, someone jokingly handed me a foil wrapped condom. Assuming I had missed the announcement (we were going to blow up balloons? Party favors?) I accepted it, but was miles from my purse, so I stuck it in my bra.

"On the way home, I decided to swing by the YMCA for some pool aerobics. I knew I'd stand out like a showgirl in the gold sequins I was wearing, so I threw a black sweater over my sparkly tank top. When I got to the locker room, it was packed with moms and little girls toweling off before trekking home. Completely forgetting my attire, I threw off the sweater and immediately one little girl seeing the sequins exclaimed, 'Look mommy, a princess!'

"Things were fine until another little girl suddenly exclaimed, 'Look mama, she has candy!' Immediately heads snapped like tree branches in an ice storm. I followed everyone's gaze to the source, only to discover—they were looking at me. What? Huh? I didn't have any candy. I looked down, and there on my right breast, in full view, was a bright purple foil packet with the word 'Trojan' in big white letters.

"In a nanosecond, the room turned from friendly to frigid. Mothers turned their backs, and instructed their children not to look. I turned to one gal who appeared to be about my age. I knew she'd understand events are rarely what they seem and there is often a logical explanation for everything.

"'Uh. I was just at a gentleman's seventy-fifth birthday party, and...' I could see the truth was not going to help in this situation. I was doomed, and the realization must have registered on my face. The woman gave me a steady gaze and in a perfect Bea Arthur/Maude voice and attitude said, 'No need to explain, 'Princess.' I think we have the picture.'"

The moral of the story, if there is one, is that humor is all around us every day, everywhere. So keep your eyes and ears open for it. You never know when its jolly head will pop up.

One of the reasons that every lesson in this book contains a Lighten-Up section is because we need to be reminded that being overly serious is not the best way to have a more joyous life. Sometimes the best way to grow, to learn, and perhaps to be enlightened is to lighten up.

I believe that all of us have a sense of humor. Sometimes it is squelched by society, sometimes by our upbringing, but we were all born with one. It is one of the mechanisms we were given as human beings to help us survive. No other animal has this unique ability to step back and get a different perspective of a situation by finding something humorous in it and then laughing about it.

The problem is that most of us forget to use our God-given gift when confronted by changes, challenges, frustrations, irritations, upsets, and all those things that aggravate us and ruin our day. We forget that humor can help us see our difficulties in a different way. So, instead of letting those annoyances take your power away, open your humor eyes and look for the funny stuff all around you.

Finding something to laugh about, particularly in trying situations, is like seeing things with a new pair of eyes or putting on sunglasses. When you put on the glasses suddenly the world takes on a different color. Green-tinted lenses make everything greener. Put on some yellow-tinted glasses and what you see seems brighter. Rose-colored lenses make the world have a pink tone to it.

Humor is like that too. One example comes from Stuart Brown's book, titled *Play*, in which he writes about his experience of standing in a long, irritating line—something that could perhaps ruin anyone's day. Brown writes about how one woman saw how long the line was and went away. When she came back later to see if the line had gotten any shorter, which it hadn't, he jokingly told her, "We all come here because we all really like hanging out here. It's a great place to spend more time."

The woman chuckled and others in line joined in the humorous bantering. "Yeah, we reconnect with old friends." "It's a great place to pick up cooking tips." "Let's take a bet on how long it will take the last person in line to make it to the pick-up window."

What started out as a long line of upset customers turned into a fun experience for everyone because Brown "humorized" the annoying situation. Instead of seeing it as a frustrating event, he saw it as a chance for some humor.

When you look at your day with a playful, humorous attitude, it's like looking at it through special glasses. You haven't changed the circumstance you are in but, with humor, what you see seems brighter and less annoying.

For more than twenty years, I have been teaching audiences worldwide how to find and use humor. My first book, *The Healing Power of Humor*, for example, has fourteen techniques for increasing your sense of humor. But even I forget about this God-given gift. So to help me to remember its availability and to learn some new ways of lightening up,

I asked some of my colleagues and fellow humorists how humor helped them be stress-free. After I completed the interviews, I noticed that there were some common traits they all employed. So here, for your enlightenment, are "The Seven Habits of Humor Gurus":

1. Be Committed.
    They were determined to get more laughter in their lives. They all made a point to find something to laugh about no matter what was happening in their life.

2. Make the Right Choice.
    They knew they had a choice: They could be miserable or mirthful.

3. Stay in Control.
    They recognized that nobody or no thing could ruin their day if they didn't let the other person, or thing, do it, which is the essence of this book.

4. Reframe the Experience.
    They turned adverse situations around by finding something funny in them.

5. Look for the Light Side.
    They were always on the lookout for the lighter side of a situation.

6. Take Yourself Lightly.

They found it mandatory to laugh at their own imperfections.

7. Laugh Even When It's Hard.

They laughed even when finding something to laugh about was not easy.

~~~~~~~~~~~~~~~~~~~~~~~~~~~~~~~

Rice, Pasta, and Potatoes

Years ago, I used to organize death and dying workshops. At one particular retreat, there were about a hundred people. All of the participants had a close connection to death. Some were hospice caregivers, some were families of terminally ill patients, and some were patients who were very near death. A few were so close to death, in fact, that they had to be carried into the meeting hall. There were also several attendees who had recently experienced the violent or sudden death of a loved one, either by suicide or murder.

The retreat lasted ten days and most of it was held in silence, except for the lectures and some personal consultations. On the seventh day, the facilitator informed me that he wanted to work with some people individually. Knowing my interest in humor and healing, he asked me to take the group over and do a session on that subject. Because of the gravity of the circumstances facing nearly everyone in the group, I was a bit apprehensive to discuss humor. But I did.

Before I tell you exactly how the group responded, you need to know one thing about the meals at the retreat. All of the food was vegetarian. Harold, who was part of the facility staff, was the cook. It was obvious from his rotund size that he really enjoyed food. He had been the cook at the center for many years and was good at what he did. But what he did was meals based mostly around meat and potatoes. This was the first time that Harold had to adhere to a strict vegetarian menu for the entire ten days. Knowing that he had little experience with this kind of cooking, we tried to clue Harold in on how to prepare well-balanced healthy vegetarian meals. We even gave him a book of vegetarian recipes. But he didn't get it. Many of his meals consisted solely of pasta, potatoes, and rice. Vegetarian, yes. Healthy, no.

The evening I was to present my discussion on humor and healing, I decided that I would give the group a multiple-choice exam. The first question I asked them was, "My favorite meal on this retreat was: A. Pasta and potatoes, B. Rice and pasta, or C. Potatoes and rice."

My opening question brought down the house. The audience laughed and howled for a long time. When the laughter died down, I asked the second multiple-choice question, "Harold's favorite food is: A. Rice, B. Pasta, or C. Potatoes."

Again the audience went wild.

By the time I got to the third question, "Your favorite retreat cook is...," all I had to do was say "A," without even revealing what the first choice was. The audience went into hysterical laughter. It was the most boisterous and receptive audience I had ever had. Later on, I realized why.

I was providing a release for them. After many days in silence and intense soul-searching, the laughter provided much-needed relief and a release of built-up tension. I also realized that the laughter that night was as important as the tears they had been crying all week.

~~~~~~~~~~~~~~~~

Follow-Up

A sense of humor can help you overlook the unattractive, tolerate the unpleasant, cope with the unexpected, and smile through the unbearable.

—MOSHE WALDOKS,
rabbi

This week, in order to have less stress in your life, and a great day every day, you might want to take a lesson from the mirth mavens mentioned above and each day incorporate one of the things they do. For example:

Day one: Commit to getting more laughter today.
Day two: Choose to be happy, no matter what.
Day three: Use humor to not let anyone ruin your day.
Day four: Find some humor in a difficult situation.
Day five: Look for the lighter side.
Day six: Laugh at yourself.
Day seven: Laugh even when there is not much to laugh about.

Lighten-Up

Laughter is like changing a baby's diaper—it doesn't permanently solve any problems, but it makes things more acceptable for a while.

—ANONYMOUS

TV personality Barbara Walters, did a story on gender roles in Kabul, Afghanistan, several years before the Afghan conflict had broken out. She noted that women customarily walked five paces behind their husbands.

Walters recently returned to Kabul and observed that women still walk behind their husbands at a respectful distance. Despite the overthrow of the oppressive Taliban regime, the women are quite happy maintaining the old custom.

Walters approached one of the women and asked, "Why do you now seem happy with an old custom that you once tried so desperately to change?"

The woman looked Walters straight in the eye and without hesitation uttered just two words, "Land mines."

TRY SMILING

⌘

*No matter who says what, you should accept it with a
smile and do your own work.*

—MOTHER TERESA,
Roman Catholic nun

I KNOW THAT it may sound basic but when things are
getting you down sometimes a simple smile can lift you up.
According to Dale L. Anderson, M.D., if you are stressed
out, "smiling can produce an immediate change of physical,
mental, and emotional states."

"Test this idea for yourself," he says. "The next time you
are feeling sad or mad, force yourself to smile. Do this no
matter how silly it seems at the moment. Then carefully
observe the resulting changes in your attitude. Notice any

subtle feeling of relaxation or relief?"

And your smile doesn't even have to be genuine. According to a study from Clark University, it doesn't matter whether you are smiling for real or faking it. A phony smile is as good for you as a real one. Either can trigger happier memories within you—and your body doesn't know the difference between a genuine one and a pretend one.

We've all heard commercial claims stating, "Nine out of ten doctors recommend..." Well I'm not sure it is nine out of ten but a number of doctors recommend that you smile more often. One prescribes two smiles a day to his patients in pain. Another encourages people to practice smiling intentionally in order to tap into what she calls "happiness hormones." And, a third, notes that even just viewing a smiling face on someone else gives the observer more life energy.

I experienced how a smile changed my day shortly after I moved from hectic New York City to mellower San Francisco. When I got on the bus one morning in my new city, the driver greeted me with a great big smile and a hearty "Good morning!" Since this never happened to me when I lived in New York I was sure he was addressing the person behind me. But when I turned around, there was no one there. The smile and the greeting were just for me and it made my day.

So, if you can't find much to laugh about this week, try smiling. It's easy. It's free. It's a great way to connect to other people. And remember, a smile is a light on your face to let someone know that you are at home.

~~~~~~~~~~~~~~~~~~~~~~~~~~~

Don't Take Your Smile for Granted

Elizabeth Usher has one of the most endearing smiles I have ever seen. But it hasn't always been that way. Because of a rare brain disorder, Beth had most of the left hemisphere of her brain removed in order to stop her agonizing seizures. As a result, she could only smile on one side. Working with two talented physical therapists for a long period of time, Beth finally got her full smile back. She says, "I love to smile and we never know when someone needs one. I love it when someone smiles back at me. It fills me with so much happiness! Remember—use your smile! Smile big and wide! It is good medicine for you and for those you smile at!"

Beth reminds us that not everyone has a smile. So don't take yours for granted and remember to treasure the one you have.

~~~~~~~~~~~~~~~~~~~~~~~~~~~

Follow-Up

He who smiles rather than rages is always the stronger.

—JAPANESE PROVERB

In Thailand, if you get angry and lose your temper, you are seen as a fool or someone who has had poor upbringing. Perhaps it is why the Thais smile in order to avoid embarrassment or to save "face." Known as the "The Land of Smiles," a grin there will get you further than a grimace or a raised voice.

Perhaps we, in Western cultures, could all take a lesson from them and smile more. Below are three ideas to help you to do that:

1. Learn a smile song and sing some of the lyrics as needed. Here are two suggestions: "When You're Smiling" or "Let a Smile Be Your Umbrella."

2. Have you ever noticed that country-western songs have a way of taking some of life's snags and turning them into something you can smile about? Take a clue from some real country song titles: "I Bought the Shoes that Just Walked out on Me." "I Went Back to My Fourth Wife for the Third Time and Gave Her a Second Chance to Make a First-Class Fool out of Me." "If the Phone Don't Ring, It's Me Not Calling You

Up." "If I Can't Be Number One in Your Life, Then Number Two on You." "She Got the Ring and I Got the Finger."

Every time you encounter some difficulty or upset this week, think of how a writer of country-western songs might turn your negative situation into a Grand Ole Opry hit.

3. If singing or songwriting is not your style there is a simpler thing you can do this week to get more smiles in your life. Post a photo on your wall or computer of someone with a great big grin. Looking at it might get you beaming too.

One more fun thing you can try. Make believe you are a scientist conducting an experiment on smiling. Every day this week, smile at everyone you pass on the street. Make a note of those who smile back at you and those who do not. In general, are they younger or older? Are they male or female? Are they suited up or dressed down? Also note how you feel when the other people don't respond to your smile, or when they do.

Lighten-Up

*You shouldn't never regret something
that made you smile.*

—BEI MAEJOR,
songwriter

One day, my friend and speaking professional colleague Karyn Buxman was giving a presentation in an unusually dark ballroom. The walls were black, the carpeting was black, and the stage curtain behind her was black.

At one point in her talk, she stepped forward, missed the edge of the stage, and found herself flat on the floor. Although she was a little startled, she realized that she wasn't hurt, just embarrassed. She also realized that the handheld microphone had fallen nearby. So, still lying on the floor, she picked up the microphone and with a great big smile announced, "And now I will take questions from the floor."

SUPERSIZE THAT

⌘

I guess I just prefer to see the dark side of things. The glass is always half empty. And cracked. And I just cut my lip on it. And chipped a tooth.

—JANEANE GAROFALO,
comedian

A CARTOON I once saw showed Jesus on a hill holding up a loaf of bread and a fish. Below him was a crowd of people calling out such things as, "I can't eat that. I'm a vegan." "Has that fish been tested for mercury?" "Is that bread gluten-free?"

One of the ways that cartoonists and comedians get us to laugh is by taking a situation and exaggerating it. For example, comic Henny Youngman said, "I was so ugly when

I was born, the doctor slapped my mother." Comedian Bill Maher, on the other hand, quips, "Los Angeles is so celebrity-conscious, there's a restaurant that only serves Jack Nicholson—and when he shows up, they tell him there'll be a ten-minute wait."

In both of the above jokes, we see the exaggerated absurdity in the comedian's overstatement and so we laugh.

This week you can do the same thing with the irritants in your life and make them less annoying. Simply take your own trials and tribulations and exaggerate them until you find some laughs, chuckles, smiles, or even a solution in them.

One such popular story, which comes from the Jewish tradition, illustrates how supersizing a situation can open doors to resolving it:

"Rabbi," said the man. "My house is so small. With my wife, my children, and my in-laws living in one room, we are always getting in each other's way. We are always yelling at one another. I don't know what to do."

The rabbi asked the man if he owned a cow. The man said he did. So the rabbi told him to move it into the house.

The man did as he was told but returned a week later to complain that things were even more crowded than before. The rabbi told the man to also move his two goats into the house. Again the man obeyed but returned to say that the situation was worse.

The rabbi then asked the man if he had any other animals. The man replied that he had two dogs and some chickens. Again, the rabbi told him to move the animals into the house.

This time when the man returned, he was livid. He complained, "It is unbearable. I'm going out of my mind. Please, please help me."

"Listen carefully," said the rabbi. "Take all the animals out of the house and come back to me in a few days."

When the man returned, he was overjoyed. "With only my wife, my children, and my in-laws in the house, there's so much room. What an improvement!"

~~~~~~~~~~~~~~~~~~~~~~~~~

Please Hold...

"Click *here* for the fun of clicking.

"Click *here* to see an image of a hand with its index finger pointing.

"Click *here* 100 times for carpal tunnel syndrome.

"Click *here* 1,000 times really fast to sound like a cricket.

"Click *here* if you want to donate a cup of rice to a poor child.

"Click *here* for the poor child's address and a map so you can find your way to the poor child's house and give him or her their cup of rice.

"Click *here* if you'll be bringing a salad or side dish."

—Marc Jaffe,
comedy writer (attributed)

~~~~~~~~~~~~~~~~~~~~~~~~~

Follow-Up

Plastic surgeons are always making mountains out of molehills.

—DOLLY PARTON,
entertainer

Every day this week, identify one thing that irritates or annoys you. Then exaggerate it until you find it funny.

You can do this by taking a bad situation, and, in your mind, make it worse. Then take the worse situation and make it even more severe. Continue to repeat that until it becomes ludicrous and laughable.

For example, you might start with: "I'm really upset because my boss won't give me a raise."

What is the worst thing that could happen if you don't get a raise?

"I won't have enough money to live on."

What is the worst thing that could happen if you don't have enough money?

"I won't be able to eat out."

What is the worst thing that could happen if you can't eat out?

"I will lose weight."

What is the worst thing that could happen if you lose weight?

"I'll get too thin."

What is the worst thing that could happen if you get too thin?

"I'll look like a string bean."

What is the worst thing that could happen if you look like a string bean?

"My clothes won't fit."

What is the worst thing that could happen if your clothes don't fit?

"I'll have to buy new clothes."

What is the worst thing that could happen if you have to buy new clothes?

"I can't buy new clothes because I didn't get a raise. So I'll have to go naked."

What is the worst thing that could happen if...

Lighten-Up

He's the type who makes mountains out of molehills and then sells climbing equipment.

—IVERN BALL,
(attributed)

A woman picked up several items at a discount store. When she got up to the checker, she learned that one of her items had no price tag. The checker got on the intercom and boomed over the loud speaker, "Need price check on lane eleven for Tampax, supersize."

That was bad enough, but somebody at the rear of the store apparently misunderstood the word "Tampax" for "thumbtacks."

In a businesslike tone, a voice boomed back over the intercom. "Do you want the kind you push in with your thumb or the kind you pound in with a hammer?"

PART FIVE

WRAP-UP

I may not have gone where I intended to go, but I think I have ended up where I intended to be.

—DOUGLAS ADAMS,
author

WRITE A LOVE LETTER

⌘

A true love letter can produce a transformation in the
other person, and therefore in the world. But before it
produces a transformation in the other person, it has
to produce a transformation within us.

—THÍCH NHẤT HẠNH,
Zen Buddhist monk

A COUPLE OF years ago, I was a guest on the Internet radio show, *Love Letters Live*, hosted by Janet Gallin. At the end of the interview, Gallin asked me to whom I would write a love letter. Numerous people came to mind: my wife whose early demise inspired a rebirth in me; my daughter and my spouse, both who continually bring me joy and laughter; my cousin who showed me how to live life fully. I also thought about my aunt who taught me about generosity in spite of her raising two kids alone and being on welfare, or the readers who have purchased my books and supported my writing and my work. Woody Allen who continually makes me laugh; my loving and caring friends; my teacher who got me into Yale Drama School; my professor who kicked me out of Yale Drama School, which spurred me on to work even harder. And those are only a few.

Yes, this is a long list of people who have enriched my life immensely and therefore warrant a love letter. But what was an eye-opener for me in the process was the importance of thanking people throughout my life, even those who may have been the biggest irritants, like the Yale Drama School professor. Ironically, it's the irritating people who can teach us the most.

As noted in a previous Wake-Up Call, expressing thanks for the not-so-great stuff in our life can be a powerful way of helping us heal a hurt. Writing a love letter can do that too. Instead of focusing our attention on what we don't have, gratitude forces us to look at what we do have. Instead of looking backward, it encourages us to look forward. Instead of bringing us down because things didn't go the way we wanted them to, being thankful and expressing it through a love letter lifts us up.

And if you think expressing your love, in a letter or otherwise, can't make much of a difference, take note of what David R. Hawkins says in his book, *The Eye of the I*, which deals with advanced stages of consciousness. He notes that just one loving person can alter the world in a dramatic way: "One individual who lives and vibrates to the energy of pure love and reverence for all of life will counterbalance the negativity of 750,000 individuals who calibrate at the lower weakening levels."

So counteract any negativity you encounter today with love. As self-help author Bryant McGill reminds us, "Hate controls everything it touches, but love sets everything it touches free."

~~~~~~~~~~~~~~~~~~~~~~~~~~

A Verbal Love Letter

My daughter Sarah, who is now 47 years old, has taught me a lot about lightening up. We have always been, and still are, very playful with each other and laugh a lot together. We could, for example, walk down the street and use the parking meter as a microphone, or, make up a gibberish foreign language and speak to each other that way on a crowded downtown street.

When I was writing my first book, *The Healing Power of Humor*, I would close my office door and use earplugs to avoid being disturbed. At the time, Sarah was in her early teens. She would often knock on the door and enter before I could respond. Usually she wanted to talk about something that could have easily waited until I took a break.

After she had interrupted me several times one morning, I put a big sign on the door that read: "Do Not Disturb Unless It's an Emergency."

No sooner than I posted the sign outside the door, there was another knock. This time I was really annoyed and shouted in disgust, "Is this an emergency?"

"Yes," she replied emphatically.

"O.K.," I angrily shouted back without opening the door. "What do you want?"

She said, "I forgot to tell you I love you."

Tears welled up in my eyes as I realized that I was taking my writing and myself too seriously. What irony! Here I was writing a book about humor and I had lost mine. It took my young daughter to remind me about love and about lightening up.

Follow-Up

*What a lot we lost when we stopped writing letters.
You can't reread a phone call.*

—LIZ CARPENTER,
American writer

Who would you write a love letter to? They can be alive or not. They can be people you know well or hardly at all. They can be people who encouraged you and those who didn't. They can be about the bad weather or the good times you had. They can be to things or to places. Your letter can be addressed to whomever or whatever you like.

Every day this week, think of one person or place to whom you might write a love letter. Then, depending on how much time you have, at the end of the week, write to at least one of them. You can mail it or not, that is up to you. Just make sure you write it.

In addition to the love letter, you might also want to consider answering the following question when someone is seemingly ruining your day. (I say "seemingly" because, if you follow the ideas in this book, you are the only one who can actually ruin your day.) What choices would you make if you came from a totally loving place in response to someone who was annoying you instead of an angry place?

Lighten-Up

*On the very same day that I ordered an iPad2, I went
shopping to buy myself a letter opener. I like to cover
all my bases.*

—SUSAN ORLEAN,
journalist

A man living in Minnesota left the snow-filled streets of Minneapolis for a vacation in Florida. His wife was on a business trip and was planning to meet him in Miami the next day. When he reached his hotel he decided to send his wife an email.

Unfortunately, when typing her email address, he missed one letter, and his email was directed instead to an elderly preacher's wife whose husband had passed away only the day before. When the grieving widow checked her email, she took one look at the monitor, let out a piercing scream, and passed out. Her family rushed into the room and saw this short letter on the screen:

Dearest,

Just want you to know that I've arrived and got checked in. Everything is prepared for your arrival tomorrow.
Love,
Your hubby
P.S.: Sure is hot down here.

PAT YOURSELF ON THE BACK

⌘

A pat on the back is only a few vertebrae removed
from a kick in the pants but is miles ahead in results.

—ELLA WHEELER WILCOX,
author and poet

WHILE WE ARE talking about love letters, don't forget that you deserve one too.

Chances are that during this week you probably encountered someone or something that felt like it was ruining your day. And maybe it did. Hopefully you did the best you could to prevent that and maybe it still happened. Not to worry. I can almost guarantee that down the road you will have another test of your "you-can't-ruin-my-day" skills. For now just know that you did the best you could under the circumstance. You deserve a pat on the back. In fact, why not make that a standing ovation?

My friend and colleague Matt Weinstein, who I mentioned earlier, was the first one to turn me on to standing ovations. He uses them in his workshops to reward people who have had a rough week. Weinstein says, "We often take for granted all the wonderful things we accomplish during the day. Sometimes we just need a boost of support to get us through a tough time."

Many of us have less trouble giving praise to others than accepting it for ourselves. Many of us believe that it is not O.K. to say nice things about ourselves. And, when we do say those things, we are frequently accused of having "a big ego." So instead of giving ourselves accolades for who we are for our accomplishments, or accepting them from others, we push them aside. Even when someone else praises us for what we have done, we often respond, "Oh, that was nothing."

Each of us has a special something within that we need to let out and let shine. So don't be shy. To celebrate this week, pat yourself on the back and remind yourself of one thing you did during each day that made you proud, or, as Weinstein reminds us, for just being you. "You deserve to be acknowledged," he says, "simply for being who you are! Don't worry about whether you've 'earned' it. Just take it in! So give yourself...a standing ovation."

Follow-Up

*No matter what age you are, or what your circum-
stances might be, you are special, and you still have
something unique to offer. Your life, because of who
you are, has meaning.*

—BARBARA DE ANGELIS,
author and speaker

Having been on a diet myself last year, I love what Steve
Maraboli writes about in his book, *Life, the Truth, and Being
Free*, when he advises, "Get off the scale!"

"Day after day, countless people across the globe get on
a scale in search of validation of beauty and social acceptance," says Maraboli. "Get off the scale! I have yet to see a
scale that can tell you how enchanting your eyes are. I have
yet to see a scale that can show you how wonderful your hair
looks when the sun shines its glorious rays on it. I have yet
to see a scale that can thank you for your compassion, sense
of humor, and contagious smile. Get off the scale because I
have yet to see one that can admire you for your persever-
ance when challenged in life."

He continues, "It's true, the scale can only give you a
numerical reflection of your relationship with gravity. That's
it. It cannot measure beauty, talent, purpose, life force, possibility, strength, or love. Don't give the scale more power than
it has earned."

With that in mind, remind yourself today to not only get off the scale but also to celebrate your successes, both past and current; to spend more time with friends and loved ones; to focus on the joyous things in your life.

Reward yourself today by eating your favorite food or going to your favorite restaurant; by wearing or purchasing something special; by going to a spa or taking a day off from work or household chores.

Remember: You deserve it.

Lighten-Up

When someone throws up while watching one of your movies, it's like a standing ovation.

—ELI ROTH,
horror film director

Burnt the dinner? Ask for a standing ovation.

Forgot to pick up the kids at school? Ask for a standing ovation.

Caused the copier to jam again? Ask for a standing ovation.

And if no one gives you one, Playfair, the company owned by Matt Weinstein, makes it easy to give yourself a standing ovation, or "Standing O" as he calls it, anytime you want one. Simply use this link and enjoy: playfair.com/standingO/standingO.htm.

LIVE AS IF YOU ARE GOING TO DIE TOMORROW

⌘

Remembering that I'll be dead soon is the most important tool I've ever encountered to help me make the big choices in life. Because almost everything—all external expectations, all pride, all fear of embarrassment or failure—these things just fall away in the face of death, leaving only what is truly important.

—STEVE JOBS,
entrepreneur

RECENTLY THERE WAS a story in the newspaper about a pet chimpanzee that attacked a friend of the woman who owned the pet. The owner was not charged in the mauling case because the attorney felt that the woman did not know the danger the animal posed. Although this is a sad story, what is interesting is that the woman who was attacked holds no ill will against her friend. According to the mauled woman's lawyer, "Her focus is on what is the next step. And going back to the incident or wishing for prosecution is a step in the opposite direction."

Along these same lines, Rabbi Harold S. Kushner, in his book *When Bad Things Happen to Good People*, suggests that when tragedies occur in our life, we need to stop asking questions such as, "What did I do to deserve this?" or "Why did this happen to me?" These are questions, he says, which focus on the past and on the pain. Instead, he says, we need to concentrate on the future and ask questions like, "Now that this has happened, what shall I do about it?"

Life is not perfect. It is filled with imperfections and things we can't control. Bad things, indeed, do happen to good people. And there is not much we can do about them. But focusing on "Why me?" takes you away from putting your energies into "What now?" It stops you and, at the very least, slows you down from partaking fully in life.

One response to why seemingly terrible things happen might be that there really is no "why." They just happen and because of their randomness our lesson from them needs to be to embrace life fully. None of us knows how much time we have remaining on this planet.

For the 2,819 people who were killed in the 9/11 attacks, it was their last day. But for a number of others who worked at the World Trade Center because they didn't go about their usual routine, it wasn't.

For example, the head of one company, who had offices in the Twin Towers survived because he took his son to his first session of kindergarten that morning. Another person wasn't killed because it was his turn to stop and get donuts. One woman's alarm clock didn't go off. A man was delayed because of an accident on the New Jersey Turnpike. Someone else's car wouldn't start. Another missed the bus. Another couldn't get a taxi.

And then there was the man who walked to work that morning in a brand-new pair of shoes. He developed a blister and stopped at a drugstore to buy a bandage. That is why he is alive today. A blister saved his life.

So, every day this week, live as if it were your last one on earth. While the thought of the possibility of this being your last twenty-four hours might seem depressing, it is also enriching. It will give you pause when someone angers you and you are tempted to chew his or her head off. It will hopefully allow you to be less harsh on yourself. Maybe you'll think differently on those days when things seem to be going wrong...when you are stuck in traffic...when your kids are slow getting dressed...when you can't find your car keys...when you miss the elevator...when _____ (fill in the blank).

The Five Regrets of the Dying

Bronnie Ware worked as a palliative care nurse in Australia for many years. From that experience she has gathered what the dying wished they had done in life but didn't. She wrote about them in *The Top Five Regrets of the Dying*.

1. "I wish I'd had the courage to live a life true to myself, not the life others expected of me."

   This was the most common regret of all—unfulfilled dreams.

2. "I wish I didn't work so hard."

   This came mostly from men, but women expressed this too—devoting too much time to work and not enough time to loved ones.

3. "I wish I'd had the courage to express my feelings."

   Many people developed illnesses related to their bitterness and resentment because they couldn't deal with their anger in a constructive way.

4. "I wish I had stayed in touch with my friends."

   Money or status were not the most important things at the end of life—love and relationships were.

5. "I wish that I had let myself be happier."

Many did not realize until the end that happiness was a choice—they longed to laugh and have silliness in their life again.

I share the above five regrets of the dying to help you sort out what is important in your life and perhaps what you need to change so that you can have a regret-free week, this week and every week after this one.

~~~~~~~~~~~~~~~~~~~~~~~~

Follow-Up

Read the obituary columns occasionally, and you'll be alerted to how trivial someone's press-worthy achievements seem after death. One example that comes readily to mind: When the "pioneer of Tex-Mex cuisine" died, the obituary column noted his two main achievements in life—having created a crisp taco shell and smothering his enchiladas in sour cream.

—SOL GORDON AND HAROLD BRECHER,
Life Is Uncertain...Eat Dessert First!

One of the founders of the *Saturday Review of Literature*, Christopher Morley, once noted, "If we all discovered that we had only five minutes left to say all that we wanted to say, every telephone booth would be occupied by people calling other people to stammer that they loved them."

Today it would not be telephone booths because there aren't many of those around. Today it would be cell phones. And no matter which carrier you have, all the lines would be jammed.

Imagine that today is your lucky day. Instead of only five minutes to live you have twenty-four hours. How would you treat everyone you encountered? Would you even bother to yell or get upset with anyone knowing that this was the last time you would be seeing them?

John E. Welshons, the spiritual teacher previously mentioned, says one practice he does every day during his morning meditation is to remind himself, "Today may be my last day on Earth—or the last for someone I love. In light of that, how do I want to spend this day? How do I want to treat people? What do I want to fill my mind with? Do I want to be loving or cranky? Caustic or kind? Selfish or generous? Fearful or peaceful?"

There is an excellent chance that this is not the last day of your life. Still, imagine how different your day would be if you knew it were. Certainly you would not let anyone ruin it. Why not go through each day this week as if it was your last day on earth and see, with that frame of mind, what happens?

Lighten-Up

*It's not that I'm afraid to die. I just don't want to be
there when it happens.*

—WOODY ALLEN,
comedian

The American comedian George Carlin had a lengthy mono-
logue about death in his act. Here is part of it:

"There is a two-minute warning [just before you die]
and I say use those two minutes. Entertain. Uplift. Do something. Give a two-minute speech. Everyone has a two-minute
speech in them. Something you know, something you love.
Your vacation, man...two minutes. Really do it well. Lots of
feeling, lots of spirit, and build wax eloquent for the first
time. Reach a peak. With about five seconds left, tell them,
'If this is not the truth may God strike me dead!'"

REMEMBER: ENDINGS ARE ALSO BEGINNINGS

⌘

When one door closes, another opens. But we often look so regretfully upon the closed door that we don't see the one that had opened for us.

—HELEN KELLER,
blind and deaf author

I WAS BORN and raised in New York City. I never owned a car there because I never needed one. So I never learned to drive. When I got married and moved to California, we bought a car. But I still didn't drive. My wife was the designated driver whenever we went somewhere.

For several months after my wife died, I looked at the car sitting idly in the driveway. Finally, one day I realized that I had three options: One, I could let it sit there and rust. Two, I could sell it. Or, three, I could learn to drive.

I chose the last option and I was glad I did. Without that skill I could never have had a career traveling around the country to present keynote speeches and seminars about my most passionate subject, the value of therapeutic humor.

What I initially saw as the painful ending to one major part of my life, the death of my wife, turned out to be an entirely new and exciting chapter that I never imagined or expected.

You may have also noticed that in your life.

Look back at your past at those painful times, those times of anguish or times of loss. Chances are you now see them differently. If some time has passed since they occurred, hopefully you have moved on, understand a little more about yourself and your resilience, and hopefully have learned from them. And, if nothing else, in spite of the pain, perhaps on some level your life is richer because of them.

Like life's cycle of life and death, you have come full circle in this book. At the beginning, there were perhaps things you did not know. Now, at the end of the book, hopefully you are richer by having some new tools to help you be happier in this sometimes not-so-happy world.

But, unlike life, this is not really the end. It is the beginning of a new phase in your life. If you have read any parts of this book and have taken them to heart, you now know some ways to not let anyone or anything ruin your day or your life.

Go forth and use them.

~~~~~~~~~~~~~~~~~~~~~~~~~~

Living Life Backwards

"I think the life cycle is all backwards. You should die first, get it out of the way. Then you live in an old age home. You get kicked out when you're too young, you get a gold watch, you go to work. You work for forty years until you're young enough to enjoy your retirement! You go to college, you do drugs, alcohol, you party, you have sex, you get ready for high school. You go to grade school, you become a kid, you play, you have no responsibilities, you become a little baby, you go back into the womb, you spend your last nine months floating.... You finish off as a gleam in somebody's eye."

—Sean Morey,
comedian

~~~~~~~~~~~~~~~~~~~~~~~~~~~

Follow-Up

Ends are not bad things, they just mean that something else is about to begin. And there are many things that don't really end, anyway, they just begin again in a new way. Ends are not bad and many ends aren't really an ending; some things are never-ending.

—C. JOYBELL C.,
author

On a piece of paper, or on your computer, write down a few things that have recently ended or will be ending soon. Then, next to each one, write down some new door that might open for you as a result of that ending. For example, your child is going off to camp for two months this summer. Instead of feeling lonely, what might you do with the extra time on your hands that will lift you up? Perhaps you could volunteer at your favorite charity, get a part-time job, or read the books you have been setting aside all year.

O. K., start writing your own ending/beginning list.

And while we are talking about endings, have you ever tried writing your own eulogy? If not, I would highly recommend it. It will show you how you would like to be remembered. And if there are things that come up that you would not like people to say about you after you are gone that's good news. You are still here so you can change those things starting right now.

Lighten-Up

The end of THE END is the best place to begin THE END, because if you read THE END from the beginning of the beginning of THE END to the end of the end of THE END, you will arrive at the end.

—LEMONY SNICKET,
pen name for American writer Daniel Handler

WIND-UP

⌘

How would your life be different if
no one or nothing was against you?

—ANONYMOUS

A LOT OF what is in this book is from my own experience, of how I see the world. I hope you will take what I've experienced, and learned in my life, and try it on for size in your life. I also realize that some of it may fit you, some may not. So I invite you to take what feels right and leave the rest.

I know too that we can't live other people's experiences; we've got to learn things for ourselves. If you want to grow, you need to step out of your comfort zone. I therefore encourage you to try on a few things that you have never tried or thought about. As various teachers have reminded me, "If you always do what you have always done, you will always get what you have always gotten."

And, one last thought: I love how author Richard Bach concludes his book, *Illusions*. He writes: "Everything in the book may be wrong."

I'd like to add one word to his thought to end this book: "Ditto."

ACKNOWLEDGMENTS

Since this book consists of a lifetime of learning, it would be impossible to acknowledge all who, in one way or another, contributed to it. There are a few, however, who have been instrumental in bringing it to fruition. Among them are Brenda Knight and the Viva Editions staff who continue to support and amaze me with their dedication, knowledge, and passion for the world of publishing. Jim Gebbie, editor extraordinaire, who painstakingly reviewed the manuscript before it was sent off to the publisher. Unity San Francisco, my spiritual community that not only brings me joy but also teaches me about the great abundance in the world. And that abundance is made richer by having my beautiful daughter, Sarah, and my loving lifelong partner, Dave, in my life. For all of them and so much more, I am grateful.

ABOUT THE AUTHOR

 ALLEN KLEIN is an award-winning keynote speaker and bestselling author. He is a recipient of a Lifetime Achievement Award from the Association for Applied and Therapeutic Humor, a Certified Speaking Professional designation from the National Speakers Association, a Communication and Leadership Award from Toastmasters International, and he is an inductee in the Hunter College of The City University of New York Hall of Fame. He is also the author of twenty-five books including *The Healing Power of Humor, Learning to Laugh When You Feel Like Crying, The Art of Living Joyfully, Change Your Life!*, and *Having the Time of Your Life*.

For more information about Klein's books or presentations, go to allenklein.com or contact him at humor@allenklein.com.

~~~~~~~~

The most important decision we make is whether we believe we live in a friendly or a hostile universe.

—ALBERT EINSTEIN,
physicist